Here's what other people are saying about

In Pursuit of Success

"If you're in pursuit of success, you must get a copy of *In Pursuit of Success*! It's the show-you-how-to-succeed book of the year!"

> —Mark Victor Hansen, co-author of #1 *New York Times* Best-selling *Chicken Soup for the Soul* series

"For those who choose to make progress on purpose...to transcend mediocrity...to achieve fulfillment...*In Pursuit of Success* is must reading!"

> —Robert Weber, author of *The Self Concept and Success, or How to Kiss Frogs Without Getting Warts on Your Lips*

"Joe B. Hill is a man who is wise beyond his years. The simple truths in this book are the keys to a successful life, if you will only decide to apply them."

> —Joe Black, speaker, trainer, author of three books, including *The Attitude Connection* and *Focus on Quality*

"If ever there was a 'believe in yourself' book, this is it! This book helped me look inside myself to realize that I'm the one that can make success happen for me."

> —Teresa Levinson, Senior Editor, *The American Salesman*

"Rarely does a book come along that can make a dramatic and positive impact on your life and your career... Joe Hill's book, *In Pursuit of Success*, is one of those rare books."

> —Marvin Young, Sales Manager, *Atlanta Coffee Time*

"Powerful and thought-provoking material for those of us who wish to be on top. *In Pursuit of Success* is the most influential self-help book that has come along in years!"

> —Mike Bacidore, Executive Editor, *Sales and Marketing Strategies & News* magazine

More Praise for...

"In this interesting, well written and remarkably wise book, Joe Hill challenges and encourages us to take an honest look into our lives and thoughts to find out what hasn't worked and why. I loved it! I'm reading it again as a reminder to myself that profoundly universal principles are also, in the living, very practical."

—Michael Misita, author of *How to Believe in Nothing and Set Yourself Free*

"Unbelievable! One of the best books I have ever read! This is a book that no one should be without—read it!"

—Mike Sevenau, author of *How to Swim with the Sharks When the Water's Polluted, or How to Succeed in Sales When Your Product Stinks*

"Joe Hill's new book, *In Pursuit of Success*, dishes up a healthy serving of soul food for anyone with an appetite for success at home and on the job!"

—Michael DeSenne, Senior Editor, *The Employment News*

"Joe Hill's been there and done that. Now you can benefit from his wisdom, experience, courage and guidance. To move to the head of the class and to get the most out of your life, you've got to read *In Pursuit of Success*. It's the secret weapon that will motivate you to take action, use your talents and follow your dreams!"

—Joyce Restaino, prestigious editor, writer, and teacher

"Joe has definitely learned what it takes to be successful—he unselfishly and modestly shares his knowledge with the reader. A great read for all of us!"

—Thomas Crowell, author of *Simple Selling*

"What a book! This guy knows his stuff—when he talks, people listen!"

—Bob Merrick, author of *The Stand Alone Inventor*

In Pursuit of Success

"Joe Hill is a marvel to observe—non-stop physical and mental activity."

— Bill Goss, author of *The Luckiest, Unlucky Man Alive*

"Too many people sabotage their own success. Don't let it happen to you. Take Joe's insight to heart and DO something!"

— Dianna Booher, author of *10 Smart Moves for Women Who Want to Succeed in Love and Life* and *Communicate with Confidence*

"Read the book; it's awesome! I learn something from it every time I read it!"

— Alvin Donovan, author of *Make More Money Now*

"A masterpiece of inspiration and motivation—clearly and constantly outlines the requirements for anyone to be successful."

— Ken Varga, author of *How to Get Customers to Call, Buy & Beg for More*

"*In Pursuit of Success* helps us clear away our mental cobwebs and polish up our possibilities."

— Joy Krause, author of *Spring Cleaning for the Soul*

" 'Life is a highway. The enjoyment you get depends upon the lane you choose,' is a quote I often use on programs. Joe Hill takes you to the entrance ramp and his book brings you quickly up to speed."

— John Furhman, speaker/trainer, author of the bestseller, *Reject Me—I Love It!*

"An honest, unbridled look at many of the things it takes to become successful, beginning with the genuine belief in oneself and the ability to turn adversity into advantage. Joe Hill speaks from the heart!"

— John Murphy, author of *Reinvent Yourself*

"If you read and heed this book, it will not take you to the top of the hill—it will take you to the top of the success mountain."

— Jeffrey Gitomer, author of *The Sales Bible* and *Customer Satisfaction Is Worthless, Customer Loyalty Is Priceless*

In Pursuit of Success

Strategies for Turning
the Obsession for Success
into a Possession for Life!

Joe B. Hill

FRIEDMAN/FAIRFAX

P U B L I S H E R S

A FRIEDMAN/FAIRFAX BOOK

© 1999 by Joe B. Hill

Library of Congress Cataloging-in-Publication data available upon request.

ISBN 1-56799-874-7

1 3 5 7 9 10 8 6 4 2

For bulk purchases and special sales, please contact:
Friedman/Fairfax Publishers
Attention: Sales Department
15 West 26th Street
New York, New York 10010
212/685-6610   FAX 212/685-1307

Visit our website:

http://www.metrobooks.com

Bring Joe B. Hill to your next meeting or convention!

Call 888-792-5462 or fax 904-321-2872

Visit Top of the Hill website at www.seenatthetop.com

Excerpt from *How to Believe in Nothing & Set Yourself Free* by Michael Misita, © 1994 by Michael Misita. Published by Valley of the Sun Publishing, Box 38, Malibu, CA 90265-0038

Excerpt from *The Rhythm of Life* by Richard Exley, published by Honor Books. © 1987

Excerpt from *Success* by Michael Korda © 1997 Ballantine Books

Excerpt from *Artful Work* by Dick Richards © 1995. Published by Berrett-Kohler Publishers

"Happy Man's Creed" and other quotations reprinted with the permission of Simon & Schuster from *Success Through a Positive Mental Attitude* by Napoleon Hill and W. Clement Stone Copyright © 1960 by Prentice-Hall, Inc., renewed 1988.

Excerpt from *What They Don't Teach You at Harvard Business School* by Mark H. McCormack. Published by Bantam Doubleday Dell. © 1988 Used with permission of International Management Group.

Excerpt from *The Luckiest, Unlucky Man Alive* by Bill Goss. © 1997 William A. Goss

Contents

Dedications/Acknowledgments

My thanks go out to these people who have made a difference in my life:

My brother, Chip, and my sister, Denise, for believing in me and my abilities to help other people.

My father, for his guidance and for being a positive role model for me to learn from.

My mother, for her support and patience.

My aunt, Mary Curtis, for the love and for the support that she gave to me unselfishly, even when I did nothing in return.

My friends Nick, Charlie, Cindy, and the many others for being my friends. They listened to me and befriended me many times when no one else on the planet would.

My friend and confidant Ben Lyles, for pushing me to do my best and befriending me.

My wife, Pat, who has stood by me and loved me through my pursuit of success.

Mr. John Heesch, who taught me several lessons and who helped me at a critical time in my life apply many of the most important lessons of successful living, when I had nearly given up on ever achieving success at anything. Among these lessons were to believe in myself and my abilities, to help other people, to trust other people, to understand what friendship really is, and not to be afraid of going after my dreams and my goals. Also, thanks for teaching me how to ride a motorcycle at deathly speeds through the Black Hills of South Dakota.

To the scores of people who helped me put this book project together. I feel certain that without their help, I may never have been able to finish this book. Thanks also to the following: Dan Poynter and his book, *The Self-Publishing Manual, How to Write, Print and Sell Your Own Book*; John Kremer and his book, *1000 Ways to Market Your Book*; Lighbourne Images for their cover design expertise; and my faithful clients.

Introduction

I have spent many hours pondering what I really want to write in this section, so that it may add to the contents of this book and to my life's thoughts, beliefs, findings, and adventures regarding success.

As I finally began to formulate the words that are written on the following pages, I realized that this book is as much for me as it is for you. I think it has been my way of "cleansing" and "releasing," if you will, my conscious thoughts, and it has given me the opportunity to live on through the printed pages of this book, no matter what happens to the physical me.

Finishing this book was something that I had to do. I recommend writing to everyone reading this book as a way of releasing your thoughts—it's worth the time. Cleanse your mind and release the thoughts that you feel are important; they will make you stronger.

You see, the end result of utilizing the strategies, beliefs, and values written on the pages of this book represents a new way of life for me. No longer will I be a simple product of a typical dysfunctional family, crooked government, and negative environment.

How will you live the rest of your life?

Regarding success? I believe we are all pretty much the same, but those of us who are more successful than others have somehow mastered the basics of successful living: communications, relationships, fun, themselves, and their energies. Highly successful people seem to have the ability to find ways to make things easier, thus achieving success. They don't seem to perform as much mental masturbation as the rest of us, who make things harder than they already are and never really ever get what we want out of life.

Though this book does contain some "psycho-babble," you will find that the strategies and theories contained herein are consistent with the many current technologies regarding self-improvement psychology, human nature, and experience. Think of this book as a tool that will help you take shortcuts to greater success. Teach others what you learn from it.

Achieving success and happiness have been the hardest things for me to do. It's been a struggle like no other that I've faced. At times, I have been so frustrated with the process of becoming successful that I have entertained the thought of quitting everything altogether. Sometimes my blind ambition and my imagination have simply overwhelmed me. I guess that is how important being successful has been to me at times in my life.

I've learned that becoming more successful in itself implies a certain amount of change; until you are willing to change who you are and what you do, you'll always be the same, and you'll likely always have only what you have got right now. You too can achieve success and have a more fulfilling life; it is your true destiny, so get started! To finish things on time, you must start them in time to finish them.

> *The problem with being poor is that it takes up all of your time.*
> —Willem de Kooning

I have previously been a man who only talks of performing actions, like writing a book. However, I realize that I have made a tremendous transition, from a man who only talks about doing things—never really completing and following through on much of anything—to one who does exactly what he says he will do. That feels good.

As I finalize preparations to send the manuscript to my editor for final review, I am reminded of a particular incident that happened to me. It will help set the stage for this book. From this incident and others like it, I learned that it was time for me to make room for me at the top.

After working my tail off for a company I sold chemicals for, I got what I thought at the time was the big break that I was looking for. I got my first promotion into sales management. What a mistake that was! I was only 23 years old. I thought that I could take on the world. I figured that because I was a great salesman, I'd also be a great manager, right? Wrong! Anyway, I had hired a rep in Lexington, Kentucky, to sell accounts in Lexington and Louisville, Kentucky. He had not been doing well after his initial training session, so I scheduled some time to ride with him and see if there was something that I could do to help him move forward.

The training day started out like every other training day. He picked me up at my motel, and we proceeded to make sales calls while I evaluated his performance and taught him some of the "ropes" of the business. Throughout the day I began having mixed feelings as to whether or not this particular gentleman was suited for the opportunity. Things were just not clicking as they should have been. After a full day of making calls, it was time to turn around in Louisville and head back to Lexington. Keep in mind that it's about a forty-minute drive between cities. Somehow, I don't remember how, about halfway home he and I began talking about whether or not this was the right opportunity for him. As we talked, I got increasingly disturbed by even having the conversation. If he had any question about whether or not he wanted to do the job, he should have never taken the job in the first place, right? To make things worse, I had already lost one salesman in the last week, and I could not afford to lose another one. As he and I talked further, I began to get really angry about the possibility of losing another rep, which would make me look like a total schmuck to my boss and to myself.

Finally, the conversation had come to its critical point. I felt like it was time for me to find out if he was staying or quitting. So, rather than trying to communicate with this gentleman, I looked over at him and said, "Well Bob, if you can't get your sales numbers up, I guess you won't have to worry about quitting, will you? I'll have to find someone else who can do the job." What happened next was one of the many turning points in my career. I guess you could call it a wake-up call.

He looked over at me and drove about a mile or so. Not a word was said by either of us. Then, suddenly, he looked over at me with a look of anger in his eyes. I could tell that I had made him mad with my previous statement. Slowly, he began to pull over to the side of the highway. I began to wonder what was going to happen next. Was he going to punch me in the chops? Well, he did not punch me in the chops. Rather, he said, "No one threatens me like that, I quit! Get out of my car and take all your stuff with you!"

I then said, "What? You are kidding, right?" He was not kidding. In a matter of seconds, he opened his trunk, threw all of the company samples and literature out on the side of the road, and drove off. He left me standing there on the side of the highway! Getting left on the side of the road with all that stuff was bad enough. To make things worse, he left me on an old two-lane highway about twenty miles from anything or anybody. I'll never forget that incident. There I was with all those product samples as well as some literature blowing down the road, because some of it had gotten loose. What an experience!

What did I learn from that incident? Never threaten to fire someone while you are in their car on a desolate two-lane highway. What I really learned was that I was not the manager, communicator, or relationship builder that I thought I was, and that I had better quickly begin learning the strategies that make one successful. How did I finally turn my obsession for success into a possession for the rest of my life? Read on.

You may already be successful!

The question is: are you as successful as you really want to be?

What would you have to read in order for you to change your circumstances today?

You'll find it on the following pages!

CHAPTER 1

PURSUING SUCCESS BEGINS WITH HAVING STRONG BELIEFS

Do you believe that you can be successful? Well, you can! There's room for you at the top! Believe it. Internalize it. Live with it, breathe it, walk it, talk it, feel it, now *runnnnn* with it!

Becoming successful in itself begins with strong beliefs that motivate us to take action. Beliefs that make us do something. Simply believing that you can do something and believing that you can be successful at doing it is half of the battle. The other half is doing the 'something' and doing that 'something' consistently.

If your dream is to be rich, you must first believe that you can be rich. Your beliefs will then motivate you to perform the necessary actions in order for you to become rich.

What we believe about ourselves and our careers truly does dictate the level at which our capabilities begin to match our desire to achieve success. In other words, it is our beliefs—the things that we believe ultimately lead us to be excited about what we are doing—that lead us toward taking action and, ultimately, to success. "We try to believe that we will enjoy complete satisfaction once we've attained worldly things, but inwardly there is an unrelenting rebellion against this false belief."

Review & Quotes & for Your Notes

Do you believe that you can be successful? Well, you can! There's room for you at the top! Believe it. Internalize it. Live with it, breathe it, walk it, talk it, feel it, now *runnnn* with it!

Simply believing that you can do something— and be successful at doing it—is half of the battle. The other half is doing the 'something,' and doing it consistently.

If your dream is to be rich, you must first believe that you can be rich. Your beliefs will then motivate you to perform the necessary actions to become rich.

(Michael Misita, *How to Believe in Nothing & Set Yourself Free*)

For example, if I were to believe that I could run 100 miles (which I cannot), I would have begun the process of taking action on my beliefs. This action would be to actually *try* to run 100 miles. Without a belief that I could do it, I would never even think about trying to attempt it. Why would I? The same holds true regarding our beliefs in ourselves to be successful at what we are doing for our chosen career path. If you do not believe that you can be successful at what you are doing, you will find it more difficult to even *try* to be successful at it. What's the point of trying to be successful at something that you believe you either are not happy doing or are afraid of doing? None!

BELIEFS = MOTIVATION = ACTION = SUCCESS!

Consequently, I believe it is from within our beliefs that true self-motivation and success come. Our beliefs are what ignite the spark of motivation. That spark ignites and helps us to take action, which then ultimately leads to success.

Take the career of selling, for example. In order to be a successful salesperson, the salesperson must believe that his or her product will benefit his or her customer, and that the company cares about both the customer and the salesperson it employs. It is the basic belief that salespeople have in their product and their company that keeps them excited and motivated enough to perform the daily grind of selling.

Ask yourself these questions: What do I have to believe in order to make my goals and dreams

---

Sidenotes:

What we believe about ourselves and our careers truly does dictate the level at which our capabilities begin to match our desire to accomplish something.

What's the point of even trying to be successful doing something that you either are not happy doing or are afraid of doing?

BELIEFS
=
MOTIVATION
=
ACTION
=
SUCCESS!

Consequently, I believe it is from within our beliefs that true self-motivation and success come.

become real? What do I have to believe in order to succeed? Do I have to strengthen any of my beliefs in myself in order to succeed?

Those of us on this planet that do believe strongly in our ability to be successful become successful, or at least try hard enough to earn self-respect and the respect of our peers. Here are two examples of this. Think about these two people and try to imagine their positions: one is on a picket line, and the other is an Olympic athlete. They both believe strongly in what they are doing and that they can be successful, or they would not be doing what they are doing. They both have clearly defined goals and support from other people for their cause. The person on the picket line will walk that picket line in the rain or snow, if he has to, in order to prove his point. Olympic athletes will train in intense pain for hours, get a private tutor, and live away from their families, if that's what it takes to become successful. Why do they do it? Because they believe so strongly in their ability to be successful that they can and will do almost anything necessary to succeed.

How can we expect to become successful doing something that we do not believe in?

I had to believe in many things, including myself, in order to be motivated to perform the necessary actions even to write this book. If I had not believed that I could write this book, I would never have taken the action of actually sitting my fanny down and writing it.

Even the best of the best periodically lose faith, and their belief in themselves or in what they are doing diminishes. God knows that I have lost faith many times. Remember this: A loss of faith and a weakening in your beliefs is

> Our beliefs ignite the spark of motivation, which leads to action, which leads to success.

> Ask yourself this question: What do I have to believe in order to make my goals and dreams become real?

> Without a strong belief that we can be successful in ourselves and in our careers, we cannot succeed. After all, how can we expect to become successful doing something that we do not believe in?

temporary! Make it temporary, let it be temporary. In other words, don't make things worse by allowing them to go downhill for too long.

Try a simple two-step strategy to help strengthen your beliefs. Simply perform a periodical inventory of your beliefs, both in yourself and in your career.

You will find that strengthening your beliefs in who you are and what you are doing will make a dramatic and positive impact on your life and your career.

Step #1. Ask yourself this question: What do I have to believe in order to be successful? Ask yourself the question several times per day, every day. Next, find the answer to it!

Step #2. Formulate your beliefs, then strengthen them by performing the necessary actions for you to be successful. In other words, don't sit around thinking about doing something, do something! Actually doing something will make you feel like you are getting closer to becoming more successful.

CHAPTER 2

BEHOLD—A PROFILE OF SUCCESS?

If you lost your job today, would you know who you are and what you really want out of your life and your career? Would you be able to continue?

"Gotta go to work."

"I gotta make it."

"I have to be successful."

"Everyone is counting on me."

"I'll lose everything that I have if I do not make it."

I think that thoughts like these go through each of our minds at some point in our lives. But for the person that is bound and determined to become successful, these thoughts or states of mind can become a way of life. Everything begins to go downhill from there for most of us, at least it did for me. See if you can relate to the following profile:

It begins with encouragement from our families and friends.

"You can do it."

"You have to work hard to be successful."

"Just pay your dues."

I must have heard them all 100 times before. I guess it stands to reason that I can't stand to

**Review & Quotes
& for Your Notes**

If you lost your job today, would you know who you are and what you really want out of your life and your career? Would you be able to continue?

hear them today. Our society, friends, and families place such a high price on being successful that it seems that, many times, being successful is all anyone places importance upon. We forget that there is more to life than succeeding at our work and being rich in terms of wealth. Other people's expectations of us can be so high that we can rarely live up to them. With such high expectations, we are actually set up to fail before we start.

We forget that there is more to life than succeeding at our work and being rich in terms of wealth.

Think about it. People who are 'failures' don't get the attention that 'successful' people get. In our society, we as a whole place too much importance on being successful. Tell me where it says that being a failure or being unsuccessful is noble or honorable. I've rarely heard anyone say that it's OK to fail and truly mean it. If they said it, it was said to make someone feel better, all the while knowing that the statement is bull!

I mean, tell me where it says that being a failure or being unsuccessful is noble or honorable?

Successful or unsuccessful? There is no option given and none taken. In the beginning, the pursuit of success seems to be a journey or a quest to conquer in order to become successful. This can soon turn into an obsession for money, status, and power. Indulgence, obsession, and the sacrifice of everything that we love becomes acceptable. After all, everything is expendable in the pursuit of success, right? WRONG!

Our needs are not being met because we have sacrificed those things that we love, and we realize that we are not having any fun.

So, blindly plunging ahead, oblivious to our obsession with and for success, we take on our first big chance at succeeding within our chosen career. We then become disillusioned by the emptiness that we experience in our career, which makes us work even harder. Our needs are not being met. We have sacrificed those things that we love, and we realize that we

We become disillusioned by the emptiness we experience in our work, so we work even harder.

are not having any fun anymore. Our determination to be happy through riches and wealth becomes apparent to everyone around us but ourselves. LONELINESS begins to set in right here. Then, the stress of the situation overcomes us, and we crash. We leave a job or relationship because of reasons like "it was their fault," and "I did not want that job anyway."

After recovering, we move on to something else—some new job or relationship to invest our life in. We stay there until we can't take the pressure any longer, and we crash *again*. It seems like everything that we do becomes a competition with everyone else. We have to have the biggest house, the fastest car, the coolest job title, and so on. NARCISSISM becomes acceptable and everything that we do revolves around ourselves.

> NARCISSISM becomes acceptable; everything that we do revolves around ourselves.

INTEGRITY? MORALS? what do they mean? We lose our PERSPECTIVE and the meaning of many of the most important things seems to fade away. Moderation? It means weakness. "I must be able to work all day and night, or I am weak."

> We lose our PERSPECTIVE, and the meaning of many of the most important things seems to fade away.

"If I do not continue, I will not win. I will not be rich and successful."

Right here is where DEPRESSION begins to set in. It is impossible to win something you've already won; many of us are already successful, but we do not realize it. The true meaning of success has escaped us. Rather than realizing that it's the pressure to become successful that we place upon ourselves that causes us to stress out, we place the blame on our relationships, our bosses, or something else.

> It is impossible to win something you've already won; many of us are already successful, but we do not realize it. The true meaning of success has escaped us.

We quickly begin to measure our success against that of our peers. ENVY begins to take its foothold. Many more things lose their true meaning, and reality really begins to get distorted. We begin to live in our own little world of pain, somehow begging for more, as if that were the answer.

LYING, both to ourselves and to everyone else, becomes a way of life and a way of justifying a false sense of purpose and worth existence to ourselves. Our ability to be RATIONAL fades. Our lives are defined only by what we do and when we do it, not by who we are, what we can do, and what we can offer to others—we have become GREEDY.

> Our lives are defined only by what we do and when we do it, not by who we are, what we can do, and what we can offer to others—we have become GREEDY.

Though we seem to be asking the right questions, *we are getting the wrong answers!* Are you getting the wrong answers? We violate the basic laws of success; we violate the people that we love, but we do not *mean* to violate them. The feeling of GUILT has not yet set upon us, but it will soon. Right about now, we LUST for the money and attention that being rich and successful can give us.

BOREDOM begins to set in here. Something even bigger has to be accomplished in order for us to feel important and successful. We know that what we are doing is not working, but we don't set our priorities. Consequently, we lose our ability to FOCUS on what is and what was truly important to us.

We begin to realize that this is not how things are supposed to be, but we have lost our ability to FEEL the things that cause real emotion in life, such as love, fun, a good movie, good music, and good friends. These things once used to touch us deeply. We feel like we can't stop for even a minute. We fear losing our edge on the competition, and FEAR becomes a state of mind and a way of life. Why? We have not yet been successful, and we have accumulated several failures. We quickly begin to lose the HOPE of ever succeeding at anything.

The TOTALITY of our life becomes our work, and the pursuit of being successful becomes the most important thing in life to us. Yes, we achieve some marginal successes along the way; but most of them are achieved without fulfillment or anyone to share them with, except those who want what we have. So we decide to work even harder to become filthy rich, so we may buy our friends, or a spouse if we have to.

> The TOTALITY of our life becomes our work, and the pursuit of being successful becomes the most important thing in life to us.

We lose the fulfillment that LOVE once gave us and begin to alienate ourselves from our loved ones, friends, and family. Many times we lose a relationship with someone that we love— oftentimes permanently. But the loss only affects us for a short time; soon we are back in pursuit of success. We begin to wonder whether or not being successful is futile, we we question our existence and our ability to do any- thing right. As a result, we start to SACRIFICE more and more, until there is nothing left to sacrifice but ourselves.

SUICIDE—ending it all—becomes a viable alternative. That would be the easy way out, but the thought crosses our minds. Somehow, we find the will and the courage to naively push on in a life and a career that feel like HELL or worse. We then begin to live life in a desperate attempt to have material posses- sions and attention, hoping they will bring back to us the love and the friends that we need so desperately.

We experience a tremendous inner emptiness, a VOID in our life that we can no longer seem to fill with our work or our trivial successes.

We experience a tremendous inner emptiness, a VOID in our life that we can no longer seem to fill with our work or our trivial successes. We continue a desperate search for fulfillment through work. It is the wrong path to take. Then we crash again. We leave that job or relationship only to invent something else to invest our life in. We don't even know that we are doing it all wrong, until it is too late.

Which path will you take?

Which path will you take?

Once we get involved with our new idea, career, or relationship, the cycle begins all over again. We get consumed by the pursuit of success. Rather than the pursuit being a magnificent adventure, we become obsessed with becoming rich and successful again.

Does any of this sound familiar?

Each time that we crash, it sucks out of us a little more of our motivation—our will to give it our all and our will to continue—until one day we realize there is little or no self-motivation left to draw from.

Each time that we crash, it sucks out a little more of our motivation—our will to give it our all and our will to continue—until one day we realize there is little or no self-motivation left to draw from. We have used up what we have and we begin to search for someone or something that will motivate us and help us become successful.

It never fails. When junk starts coming at us and we feel like things are out of control, everything seems to pile up on us; it all becomes junk after a while. That downward spiraling process is hard to stop. It's like hitting the brakes on a train that's moving downhill. It's hard to stop the train and even harder to get the train headed back in an upward direction. Life is very much the same way.

Wanting to be successful that badly is nothing more than an endless obsession that can make you want to die. I know, I've felt this pain many times over. You see, the profile that you have just read was mine. I hope that you cannot relate to it. But if you can, this book will show you many ways to stop the endless, unsatisfying, ungrateful, demeaning, stressful, burnt-out way that we as superachievers try to achieve success.

What will your memories be like when you look back on the things that you did to become successful? How will you relate to this profile?

It is easy to lose our focus of what is really important in life. I know that I did. Have you lost your focus of what is really important to you? It is easy to spend too much time in relationships that are unhealthy, at jobs that we hate, and with people that we do not like. It's a living hell that I know quite well. I think that many of us have suffered through hateful jobs, bad relationships, and friendships with people who, in the end, are not really our friends.

Many of us also suffer from an imbalance between our work, fun, relationships, selves, and energy. We do not stop long enough to enjoy the basic things in life that can be enjoyable. We've become obsessed with becoming successful, and we'll sacrifice anything for it—even our happiness. Some might call the obsession for success a strong work ethic. I call it a way of life that leads to emptiness, loneliness, and depression.

Real progress can be made only when we finally realize that our lifestyle and our careers are not fulfilling our needs, and we become dissatisfied with the way that things are. Then and only then do most of us do anything to change things. It's silly, but most of us don't do any-

> Success is an endless obsession that can make you want to die.

> What will you look back on? What will your memories be when you look back on how you became successful? How will you relate to this profile?

> Have you lost your focus of what is really important to you?

> Many of us suffer from an imbalance between our work, fun, relationships, selves, and energy.

thing until it's too late. Until you become dissatisfied with the way that things are, you may never take a long, intuitive look into why you are unhappy or un-wealthy. Thus, nothing will change. You may still be unhappy, broke, and looking for something to fill the 'void' several years from now. Don't let this happen to you.

So, who are you, really?

Inevitably, a lifestyle of making mistakes and suffering from depression, as I did, catches up to us. For many, it becomes what has been called by others a midlife crisis, but that's not the full explanation of what is happening. It goes much deeper than that. It goes to our very heart and soul and makes us question our existence. It sometimes takes more internal courage and faith in ourselves than we really have to make our own decisions and choose our own fate. I know that I could have avoided many of my mistakes by listening more intuitively to myself. What a simple thing to do for such amazing results.

It sometimes takes more courage and faith in ourselves than we really have to make our own decisions and to choose our own fate.

In his book, *The Rhythm of Life*, which I highly recommend as excellent reading, author Richard Exley relates to the pursuit of success like this:

> Between these extremes is the called man. The one who sees himself as a steward, his life as a gift to be invested and managed for the Lifegiver, and his work as an expression of who he is. For him, work is its own reward. It's an important part of his life, but only a part. He's obedient rather than ambitious, committed rather than competitive. For him, nothing is more important than pleasing the One Who called him. Consequently he is free to balance his work with rest, worship and play. (p. 20)

I'd say that is an awesome perspective, wouldn't you?

Sometimes, the thought of just giving up seems like a viable option.

Life would be so much simpler if we'd just quit and go on welfare, wouldn't it?

I don't think so. Quitting is not what we really want to do; succeeding and becoming happy is. Are we all not in search of a fulfilling life, a healthy relationship, and a career devoid of emptiness, depression, loneliness, and narcissism? Don't we all want the strong feelings of gratification, recognition, and material wealth that seem to accompany and personify what many people perceive or interpret as 'success'? Why do we somehow find ourselves without any of these things?

If you have been at the success game long enough, you have at some point entertained the thought of quitting everything and moving to the country for a much more simple lifestyle. I went so far as to do it (or so I thought). I moved to the beach to escape from my own complications in life. As usual, I learned another lesson through experience. I realized that moving to the beach was not necessarily the entire answer that I was looking for. I also learned that moving to the beach had been overwhelmingly good for me. It served its purpose, which was to help rejuvenate my spirit and to put my life and my career into a healthier perspective.

Keep this in mind regarding a general perception of success. There is definitely more to a successful life and career than wealth, agreed? Yes? No? However, I'd rather be rich and miserable than poor and miserable!

What is your destiny?

Life and the pursuit of success would be so much simpler if we'd just quit, wouldn't it?

We fail to prioritize things in our lives and it creates an imbalance.

Here's what happens. We spend 99% of our time working at something that we think we like, but which we really only tolerate; this causes an imbalance. We spend too much time relentlessly pursuing material possessions and money rather than happiness, fulfillment, and love. Then we lose track of the other 1% of the time that we have left. I am guilty of spending too much time doing work and chasing money. Consequently, I have burned out many times. I simply failed to prioritize what is really important in my life and actually violated all of the basic laws of success. No wonder I failed miserably so many times.

Like many of you who may be reading this book, I still have my days when I want to quit everything and lie on the beach. However, when those feelings come over me, I realize that it's not quitting that I need to do; it's simply my intuitions and my conscious thinking abilities telling me to take a short break from my work and to go have some fun.

Is it any wonder why many of us are miserable? Is it any wonder why many of us are miserable?

A LITTLE STORY

I'd been selling hospital furniture for a great company based in Indiana. My territory included most of South Dakota, North Dakota, and Nebraska. That's one heck of a piece of real estate to cover, by the way. The first year alone I drove over 77,000 miles and flew I don't know how many miles. I've spent more time for ten years of my life in my car, driving around selling things, than I have doing anything else. Subsequently, I realized that I was missing much of what life had to offer me, like time to build a family, to strengthen my relationship with my wife, and to just plain have some fun. I knew I needed some balance in my life and I decided to get some as fast as I could.

I remember many times, prior to leaving my last obsessive "job," how I would pack my gear for a week-long trip on the road while saying to myself: "This is the last trip." Then, one day, something happened that helped me make the decision to leave the money, the long hours of road driving, and the loss of time; it helped me enjoy each day the way that I *wanted* to enjoy it.

I'd packed my gear for another typical week-long, 1,000+-mile trip from Rapid City, South Dakota, to Nebraska, so I could make sales calls. It was around 6:00 AM on a typical South Dakota winter morning. (If you have ever been out that way before you'll appreciate this.) It was cold, windy, and some light snow was falling. Now, there is absolutely nothing but open road out there for about 60–70 miles at a stretch, and in most places, it is farther than that. I mean nothing. No houses, no other cars, nothing! So, if you happen to have an accident out there you could easily freeze to death before someone would find you. Anyway, there I was, driving about 90 mph down this desolate old two-lane highway; I was not going to be late for my appointment, but as I'd done so many times before, I fell asleep at the wheel.

When I woke up, I was about 50 feet from a head-on collision with this trailer, and there was nowhere to bail off the road to safety. You see, the driver had merged into my lane—and I had merged into his—while I was asleep. I did not know for sure which lane he was going to stay in. Would he stay in mine, or would he swerve back into his now that he saw that I was awake. We were so close, we could see each other's facial expressions. I could see his face, and I think I actually read his lips as he said, "Oh—!" I thought I was going to die on that old South Dakota highway for sure.

Now, as miserable as I had become at that time in my life, I instantly decided that I did not want to die in a car wreck with a tractor-trailer in South Dakota. In a split second, I decided to get over as far as I could on his side of the road without running off the 25-foot drop-off and hope that we missed each other. We did pass each other. I in his lane, he in mine. Both of our faces were strained with the fear of dying. I think he read my lips when I said, "Oh—," as we passed, too!

I pulled over about two or three miles down the road and decided right then and there that I would never again take a job that made me miserable or required me to risk my life doing it just to make a buck. I decided right then and there that I was no longer going to risk my life driving across the country for a measly pay-check. I fall asleep at the wheel too much to travel by car just to make a living, anyway.

Well, I finished the trip. When I returned, I made a call to my dad and one to my wife, informing them of my decision to leave that company if it did not find me a smaller and more southern territory, like Georgia or Florida. I don't think the company took me seriously until I formally left the job. I left what most people consider to be an elite selling posi-tion, making big money with a great company.

To make things worse, my father was a legendary salesman for the same company, and I had followed in his footsteps. Tell me *that* didn't add to the pressure of the situation!

So, what do you think? Did I leave success far behind, along with some unfulfilled dreams and a list of failures, or did I stop, refocus, and move on, to become more successful than ever before?

After I left the job, I tried my turn at the music business, among other things. I also had a few other little adventures that kept me busy, but they are not worthy of even mentioning. More importantly, I was taking this time out in my life to discover some things about myself, to get to know the real me and what I really wanted out of my life and my career. I took a long, hard look at how I had done things in the past; what worked, and what did not work. I took time off for some serious reflection upon my life and my career. This book will help you do the same.

In Pursuit of Success will guide you through some things that help bridge success with achievement, and help you achieve a more fulfilling life, one filled with happiness. Yes, I guess you could say that I did it all wrong. My past led me to realize that I had lived about 28 of the now 33 years that I've been on this earth completely miserable. I was in constant pain, brought on by my lack of vision, need for acceptance, lack of intuitive understanding, and my obsession for success and material gain. Looking back on things now, I know that I gave up way too much to become successful.

The following are strategies that I learned and that turned my life and career around; they have led me to achieve my unique form of success.

CHAPTER 3

WHAT IS IT THAT MOTIVATES US—THAT DRIVES US TO BE SUCCESSFUL?

Not long ago, I met a young man in one of my favorite cigar nightspots in Cincinnati, Ohio. I happened to be enjoying a cigar and just minding my own business at the time. I don't remember how we met or how our conversation began, but eventually the young man asked me what I did for a living. I proceeded to tell him about who I was, my work as a trainer and speaker, and my plans of writing this book. He seemed to be impressed with the fact that I was not that much older than he and doing many of the things that he himself had wanted to do with his life, so we sort of hit it off.

After we had an opportunity to share some conversation, he told me that he had always dreamed of becoming a writer. Admittedly, he said that he'd probably write science-fiction books, but that he was not sure of how to do it; the entire process overwhelmed him. I could tell that his confidence in himself was very low.

I gave to him some advice that I often use myself to spark my own creativity, to renew my self-confidence, to motivate myself to take action, and to remember how easy it can be to become successful. I asked him if he really wanted to be a writer. He replied with an enthusiastic "Yes."

I remember telling him this: "Go home, formulate the outline for your book, and write the first page. After you have finished the first page, you will be a writer; it's that simple." He looked right into my eyes and said: "Yeah, you are right. All I have to do is write the first page and I'm a writer. I might not sell a lot of books and get rich, but I will be a writer, and that's what I want to be."

I told him that what he'd identified as a dream—to write a book—was easily attainable if he'd just get started doing it. I made it clear to him that he had to stop dreaming about writing it, stop making the process harder than it really is, and begin writing the first page. I then pointed out that he had not said that he wanted to write a book just to get rich with a big book contract. He'd only identified the fact that he wanted to be a writer. He then replied, "Thank you for your help; I have to go." I asked him where he was going. He said, "I have to get started on that outline and first page." He left and I never saw him again. I hope he finished his book.

The point of this little story? We make becoming successful harder than it really is. So what was it that drove or motivated that fellow to begin writing the book? I'd like to think that it was those simple words of encouragement I gave him that showed him how easy it really was to achieve his dream of becoming a writer.

Don't make things any harder than they already are.

What is it that drives you to be successful? Admiration? Self-preservation? Love? Fear? Sex? Life after death? Freedom? Hate? Recognition? Self-expression? Material possessions? Money?

Why are some people more successful than others? What is it that makes you do what you do in order for you to become successful? What can you do to sustain and nurture a high level of self-motivation?

What is it that drives you to be successful? Why are some people more successful than others? What is it that makes you do what you do in order for you to become successful? What can you do to sustain and nurture a high level of self-motivation.

The answers to these questions can only be answered by you. Through a process of intuitively clarifying and identifying what it is that really motivates you, you can intuitively and consciously make better decisions and keep yourself motivated.

In the following paragraphs, I have identified what I believe to be the five most common motivators, but it is from within our *own* beliefs and our *own* perceptions of these that our true motivation comes. I call them "The five P's." They are as follows: Pain, Pleasure, Prestige, Promotion, Paycheck.

The five P's: Pain, Pleasure, Prestige, Promotion, Paycheck.

THE FIVE P'S

The Five P's and some common misconceptions regarding each of them:

1. Pain.

Generally, the pain that we experience most often is the pain that we inflict upon ourselves, such as our fear of failure or the pressure that we place upon ourselves to perform successfully.

Too often we associate pain with motivation and success. Generally, the pain that we experience most often is the pain that we inflict upon ourselves, such as our fear of failure or the pressure that we place upon ourselves to perform successfully. Oftentimes the pain comes directly from our employers, who drive us too hard to produce measurable results.

PAIN

=

FEAR

=

MOTIVATION?

Pain = Fear = Motivation?

This is a common equation that is used to motivate people to perform successfully. It's done simply by placing us in fear of our jobs, a demotion, or a pay cut. Strangely enough, pain can be very motivating, but its effects are short term. I can relate well to being motivated by pain. For many years, I was motivated by the pain of doing things that I really did not want to do for a career out of the necessity to make a paycheck. What kind of pain is motivating you?

2. Pleasure.

I believe that our true need to receive pleasure from our lives and our careers is the best of all motivators. The problem is, many of us do not regularly seek out pleasure in our lives and our careers. We are too busy searching for everything else but pleasure. Why do we do that?

Some of us are motivated by pleasurable toys or pleasurable trips. Some simply take pleasure in having the time and the money to do whatever it is that they like to do. Whatever it is that is pleasurable and that motivates you to do your best, keep doing it! (As long as it's legal, ethical, and morally correct.) Life as a whole and the pursuit of success are supposed to be pleasurable. I have made a commitment to myself to make absolutely, positively sure that they are pleasurable for me. No matter what. Have you?

3. Prestige.

Motivation by prestige alone can be very dangerous. After all, prestige is an ego thing, one which is responsible for many failed attempts to become successful. I admit, it's nice to have a neat title like Vice President and the perks that come along with the responsibility of a job like that. But ultimately, the title does not mean a thing. After you separate the things that are really important and mean something, prestige is nothing more than a by-product, a result of being successful. It does not give us bragging

Pleasure. I believe that our true need to receive pleasure from our lives and our careers is one of the best motivators.

Keep doing whatever is pleasurable and motivates you to do your best.

Life as a whole and the pursuit of success are supposed to be pleasurable.

Prestige is an ego thing anyway, and it is responsible for many failed attempts to become successful.

Prestige is nothing more than a by-product, a result of being successful.

Being motivated
by prestige alone
constitutes and promotes
narcissistic behavior.

rights. Beware, being motivated by prestige alone constitutes and promotes narcissistic behavior. Believe me, there is no room left on the planet for another narcissist!

4. Promotion.

I'm sure, if you have been in the job market very long at all, you have been promised a promotion by someone. You know, the "dangling the carrot in your face" routine. More often than not, the promotion continues to elude most of us.

For many of us, the possibility of a promotion at work can most definitely be a motivator. A promotion usually means more money, more social status, added prestige, more toys, and undoubtedly more work. Most of these are unimportant. I believe it is the added social status and prestige that make a promotion so attractive or motivating. You see, our perception of what a promotion *really* is escapes many of us. A promotion is meant to compliment someone on a job well done. From my point of view, it's our perception of the promotion that must change.

A healthy perspective
of the 'promotion'
would not view it as
a way of showing
how much better you
are than others.

A healthy perspective of the 'promotion' would not view it as a way of showing how much better you are than other people. Rather, a promotion is an opportunity to further contribute your talents to a worthwhile career and a company that needs your expertise. Your expertise will be used to help others learn so the company and its employees as a whole can become more successful. Does the promise of a promotion motivate you? Why? Or why not?

5. Paycheck.

Money, money, money. Money is the most dangerous motivator of all. The pursuit of only money can leave us devoid of the intuitions that make us successful. Money contributes to narcissistic behavior. It will make you defy the basic success principles. If you are motivated by money, that's good. Due to our system of exchanging merchandise in this world, we must have money in order to survive and have a lifestyle that contributes to our happiness. What is bad is when money is the only thing that motivates you. Don't allow yourself to get in a position where you will do anything for money.

How does money motivate you? Would you do almost anything for money?

Money is the most dangerous motivator of all.

If you ever get to a point where you will do anything for money, you have more problems than I can help you with. Get some help.

CHAPTER 4

THE FOUR CRITICAL DECISIONS

It's time to actually make some decisions that will propel you toward success. Are you ready to make them?

I believe that there are four critical decisions that each of us must make in order to begin the process of creating unbridled self-motivation and long-term successful habits in our lives and in our careers—to be able to truly pursue success and to stop hoping, wishing, talking, dreaming, or thinking about being successful, to actually start *doing* something to become successful. These are decisions that must be made before action to ensure your success can be undertaken. These are the preliminary decisions that I believe most of the successful people on the planet have had to make before achieving real lifelong success. I had to make them myself, and most likely, if you really want to be successful, so will you.

The real question is: "Will you, can you, and are you ready to make some really tough decisions?"

The question is, will you, can you, and are you ready to make some really tough decisions that affect your life and your career?

These four critical decisions are not to be taken lightly. They will have a dramatic impact on you and may ultimately determine your level of either success or failure. When properly made, they will begin the process of helping you to stop performing the self-defeating actions that do not take you closer to your dreams and goals of being more successful. You will begin performing actions that initiate positive change.

Decision #1

Are you really ready to accept some help in order for you to become more successful?

By first purchasing and then reading this book, I believe that you have taken the first critical step toward achieving greater success. You have done something that few people ever do. You have made a simple decision to initiate a search for help. What a powerful step you have taken, and you may not even know it! Ultimately, you have made a decision to learn more about how to succeed, which is decision number one.

This is where many people fail. They do not make the kind of critical decisions that this section will help you make, and they do not question how and why things are the way that they are. Nor do they question what happens when we make the decision to actually become more successful. Don't stop here; keep going! This is exciting progress.

By answering "yes" and making a decision to ask for help, you have begun an exciting chain reaction of decisions, decisions that you have to make in order to really go after success. By answering "no" to this question, you have made no real progress. You may be making more mistakes and taking more time to be successful by doing it all on your own. Why not learn from the mistakes that other people have made and learn how not to make them? Personally, I would rather follow someone through a pasture of poop piles than be the one leading the way!

Decision #1

Are you really ready to accept some help in order for you to become more successful?

By initiating a search for help and information, you can learn from other successful people and learn how to become more successful. This way, you learn about strategies that worked and those that did not work. Thus, you will become successful much faster. Here's a tip. Don't stop learning with this book. Continue reading other books and increase your knowledge.

Decision #2

Are you dissatisfied with the way that things are right now?

At some point, you must have been dissatisfied with the way things are, or you probably would not have wasted the time and money to purchase and read this book. You see, at the single moment when you become dissatisfied with the way things are, you initiated a search for answers to a series of questions. These very important questions lead to some important decisions, decisions that you need to make in this chapter.

Have you ever said to yourself, "This job is not enough for me;" "I deserve better than this;" or "I can do better than I am doing now, but I don't know how." I believe that most of us have at some point. The problem is that too few of us actually have the courage to change the way that things are.

To move forward spiritually, emotionally, physically, or professionally from where you are right now, you must come to a point in your life or career when you will finally admit to yourself that you are dissatisfied with the way things are, and you are ready to change things. At that point, you will begin to change yourself, to change your life, to change your career, to

Decision #2

You are dissatisfied with the way that things are, and you are ready to change, aren't you?

change whatever it takes in order for you to reach the level of success you desire. You *must* realize this in order to move forward and achieve your dreams and goals. Commit to changing something right now!

If your answer is yes, you are ready to change things; you have taken the next step toward greater success, and you have made the right decision. The decision that you have made really means that you want and need more than you are getting out of your life and your career, and you are ready to change whatever you have to in order to get what it is that you want. Well done!

STOP!

If you have not made a commitment to change the way that things are, do it now! There is no guesswork to this decision; there are no maybes! Either you are ready to change what is wrong and what has not been working for you and move on or you are not!

What's it going to be? Are you ready to change the way that things are? Yes or no?

By making a yes decision, you have changed your entire destiny. You will be more successful. Your life will change for the better. If you have decided not to change something, you will have made no significant progress and things will remain as they are and have been. You'll still be hoping, wishing, thinking, talking, and dreaming about getting what you want.

Decision #3

Will you commit to setting higher standards and goals for yourself?

You must make the decision right now to set

Decision #3

Make the decision right now to set higher STANDARDS and GOALS for what *is* and what *is not* acceptable for you, and decide how you will achieve them. Have you?

higher STANDARDS and GOALS for what *is* and what *is not* acceptable for you in your life and your career, and for how you will achieve them.

When you set higher standards and goals for your life and your career, you truly begin the process of creating unbridled enthusiasm, motivation, and successful habits, because you will have thrown away forever the "limitations" and "influences" that keep you from attaining your dreams and your goals.

Many of us fail to make this critical decision, because making it does take some real soul searching to properly determine what kind of standards and goals to set for ourselves. Trust me, it's not that difficult of a decision to make. You can do it. Do not make it any harder than it already is.

Higher standards and goals? Yes. If you really do want more than you are getting out of your life and your career, you must set higher standards and goals. Higher standards for yourself to live by, and higher goals that you can achieve one step at a time.

Setting higher standards and goals for how you will live your life and what it is that you really want is critical. Without setting the ground rules now for what you want, how would you know what it was if you ever found it? Maybe you want a higher income, a better way of life, or a better and healthier relationship with a spouse. Maybe a higher standard for you would be to earn your first new car, so you've decided never again to be in a position in your life that makes you drive a beat-up used car. Maybe you want to hold yourself to higher standards in regards to how you will treat other people.

Here are some other examples of some higher standards that you may set for yourself: better housing, more money, better transportation, more respect from others, more respect for yourself, a new way of life, a commitment to physical fitness, etc. These are all good places to start when setting new and higher standards for yourself. You see, it is these new higher standards and goals you set for yourself that will allow you to break out of your comfort zones, to avoid being held back, and to move toward a direction of success.

I set new standards for how I was going to live my life and for what I wanted to do for a career. I had to because I was so unhappy with the way I had previously been living my life and I was unhappy with my career path. What I did was to identify some areas of my life and my career that I was and that I was *not* going to accept as a standard. Then I identified some things that I would be happy with—that would satisfy me. Next, I simply set new standards for what was and for what was not acceptable for each of the areas that I had identified. Finally, I set higher goals that would allow me to achieve and live up to my higher standards.

Here are four examples of the many higher standards and goals that I set for myself. Can you relate to any of these?

Identify four higher standards and goals for your life and your career.

1. I set higher standards *for my career* by making a commitment to help other people. I decided that nothing less than a position in which I could help other people was going to be acceptable to me for a career. I then set a goal to achieve my own consulting company and accomplished it.

2. I set higher standards for *the way that I live my life* by keeping myself in at least decent physical shape. No longer was it acceptable for me to be overweight and to lose the enjoyment that I receive from being physically active. I decided that I'd rather be home more often and have the opportunity

to stay fit than spending most of my life in a car making sales calls, eating doughnuts, and getting fat. I then set a goal to exercise three to four times per week and to remain in good physical shape, thus living up to my new set of standards.

3. I set new standards for *where I wanted to live*. Previously, I'd lived away from the ocean and the beach. This made me miserable, because I love them so much. I seem to draw natural and abundant energy from the ocean and the beach. So, I set higher standards for myself by making a decision to live at the beach and to enjoy the benefits that a beach and the ocean surely have to give. Anything less than living at the beach was now unacceptable. I then set a goal for when I was going to make the move to the beach. Incidentally, I moved to a Florida beach on May 30, 1997, and one of the biggest dreams of my life became a reality.

4. I also set new standards *for how I was going to treat—and be treated by— other people*. I decided that no longer was I going to let myself be narcissistic, and no longer was I going to be unfaithful to the values that I believed in. Whatever higher standards you set, live by them. Make a commitment to follow through on them.

When you set higher standards and goals for your life and career, you truly BEGIN the process of creating unbridled enthusiasm, motivation, and successful habits, because you will have thrown away forever the "limitations" and "influences" that keep you from attaining your dreams and your goals.

Here's a Critical Point

Now that you have set these higher standards and goals for yourself, you must be willing to "pay the price" up front and right now for achieving them. Are you willing to pay the price, to sacrifice right now and up front to get what you want?

You see, there is a "price" that you will have to pay, some "sacrifices" that you will have to make in order for you to achieve greater success and your dreams/goals. *This is the biggest decision that most of us do not make before we first do some intelligent and intuitive thinking.*

Many of us are real good at talking, dreaming, hoping, and wishing that we could be, do, and have more than we have right now. But, when we find out what the price for achieving these things really is—hard work, longer hours, or risk-taking—many of us wimp out and decide that what we said that we wanted is not worth the price and sacrifices that we will have to make in order to get it.

Creating long-term self-motivation and success in a life or a career doesn't "just happen"—you must create them. If what you are doing now is not working for you and making you happy, you alone must be willing to change it.

Many of us make critical decisions to pursue our dreams and our goals; we invest our life's savings, risk our health and even our relationships with our loved ones, only to find out later that the goal that we were pursuing was not going to be worth what we had to do in order to achieve it, so we quit altogether. We then sit back asking ourselves, "What happened? What went wrong?" The answer is that we did not investigate the prices and sacrifices of our

Critical Point

You must be willing to "pay the price" up front and right now for greater success. Are you willing to pay the price and to sacrifice right now and up front in order to get what you want?

dreams and goals *up front*, or commit to paying for them *up front* before pursuing them.

This kind of sporadic decision making is very common for those of us who get into new opportunities to achieve success, but then quickly get back out again because the opportunity was either not what we thought it was, or we decided that succeeding at it was going to take more than we were willing to give. This has happened to me no less than seven times to date.

Before pursuing your dreams and goals, first determine the prices and sacrifices that you'll have to pay and make in order for you to get whatever it is that you want. You will avoid many disappointments and save yourself a lot of time.

Identify Your Prices and Sacrifices Right Now!

Identify five of the sacrifices and prices that you will have to pay in order for you to get what you really want (longer hours at work, etc.).

Your prices and sacrifices may be hard work, working longer hours, making stronger commitments, spending less time now with loved ones, etc. Whatever the prices or sacrifices that you will have to pay in order to get what you want, determine them right now and make a commitment to paying them up front. Don't even bother pursuing something halfway.

Now, stop reading, use a separate sheet of paper, and identify five prices and/or sacrifices that you will have to pay in order for you to get one of the things that you really want. When you finish, return to this page and continue reading. STOP reading, start thinking, and begin writing!

Decision #4

The final decision is simple. Now that you have identified some of the prices you will have to pay in order to get what you really want, ask yourself: "Is what I want worth the sacrifices and prices that I have to pay in order to get it?" Yes or No? Are the rewards for your prices and sacrifices going to be worth the commitment it will take for you to get what you want? Yes or No? If yes, then you are on your way to getting what you want. If your answer is no, rethink this strategy, reread this chapter, and find something that is worth the price for your success.

When your answer to this question is a clear—with no shred of doubt—yes, continue reading. You are ready, willing, and able to move forward and to pursue success with fewer limitations.

Make no mistake, if you do not make these four critical decisions for yourself and your future, these decisions will be made for you! YOU must decide WHAT will, WHEN it will and WILL NOT happen to you. If you have not done this yet, DO IT NOW! You must decide right now that you will not accept anything less than what you want and deserve, that you will no longer be influenced by the very things and people that are making your life and career decisions for you, but do not take you closer to your dreams and goals for your life and career.

Decision #4

The final decision is simple. Now that you have identified some of the prices you will have to pay in order to get what you really want, is what you want worth the sacrifices and prices that you have to pay in order to get it? Yes or No?

Long-term self-motivation and success in a life or a career don't "just happen"—you must create them.

CHAPTER 5

SUCCESS AND MOTIVATIONAL MYTHS

How do you define success and motivation? I believe that it's a process of attaining clarified and obtainable dreams and goals, coupled with a conviction that binds your entire existence. It's a commitment to decisions and strong beliefs, to a lifestyle that you have made a commitment to yourself to uphold. In turn, you will accept nothing less than you deserve, than you believe that you can have. Above all other things, it's a commitment to being happy. All of this translates into successful habits and actions for one's life and career and, ultimately, success.

So much of today's information regarding how to become successful and how to motivate yourself is untrue, even mythical by nature. In this chapter, I have identified several success and motivational myths, and I have tried to debunk some of the common misconceptions for you. Believe this. There is no myth to being successful. What I do believe is that the facts on how to become more successful have been grossly distorted. Success, and the pursuit thereof, is only as difficult as we make it.

MOTIVATIONAL MYTHS

Motivational MYTH #1

MYTH: Motivation is something you do *to* someone rather than *for* someone.

FACT: It's untrue!

I am sharing my thoughts and strategies for you and your benefit. You can read this book and make your own decisions as to whether or not you will follow the strategies contained herein. I believe that motivating each other is a duty that we all have. It's up to every one of us to help each other. So, motivating someone is something that we do *for* each other, not *to* each other.

Motivational MYTH #2

MYTH: Inspiration is the same thing as motivation.

FACT: It's untrue!

Highly inspired people ultimately draw from their own inspiration to provide themselves with the motivation to continue the pursuit of success, even in the worst of conditions. So ultimately, inspiration is something that we draw either from within ourselves or from other people that may inspire us. Thus, inspiration may *mature* into motivation, but inspiration is *not the same as* motivation.

I, myself, am inspired by my desire to help others, but I am motivated by the positive responses that I get from people who want something more out of their lives than what is "ordinary," and who have either attended one of my seminars or have bought this book and have benefited from reading it. What inspires you?

Motivational MYTH #3

MYTH: Success is related to "hard work," which requires "discipline." This is the "just work hard" theory.

FACT: This is simply not true either.

There is too much information regarding how to become successful that is untrue, even mythical in nature.

I believe that there is no myth to being successful. What I do believe is that the facts on how to become more successful have been grossly distorted. Success, and the pursuit thereof, is only as difficult as we make it.

Motivational MYTH #1:
Motivation is something you do *to* someone rather than *for* someone.

Motivational MYTH #2:
Inspiration is the same thing as motivation.

It does not take discipline or hard work to be successful. It takes being highly internally and externally motivated. It takes strong beliefs that make you take action, and it takes a commitment to a lifestyle of successful habits.

You see, if we worked hard or were "disciplined," we would never smoke, drink, or get divorced. We'd lose twenty pounds of body fat; we'd never use bad language, etc. "Hard work" and "discipline" do not constitute success and motivation. They only contribute to burnout and depression.

Motivational MYTH #3:
Success is related to "hard work," which requires "discipline." This is the "just work hard" theory.

I don't believe in the "just work hard" theory. Today, you must do more than just work hard to be successful. Seemingly, the word "success" implies that we must do everything shy of killing ourselves in order to attain it. It's not true. I believe success and motivation come from believing in ourselves and what we are doing with conviction, and from consistently performing successful strategies for your life and your career. You see, it's what you do consistently—on a daily basis—that shapes your life, not what you do once in a while.

Motivational MYTH #4
Being happy with your life does not mean that you are self-motivated.

Motivational MYTH #4
MYTH: Being happy with your life means that you are self-motivated.

FACT: Just because you are happy with yourself and your position in life doesn't mean that you are highly motivated. I've personally known some very happy people, so "happy" that they never got a real career opportunity or did anything with their lives. They wasted their talents. They began to accept what was happening to them (which was nothing special) and they began to "coast" through life.

What has really happened to many of them is this: they have secretly given in to the pressures of the pursuit of success. They are tired of wanting more and not getting it. I've been there many times. I finally got tired of getting kicked in the butt, and I started doing the kicking! Are you tired of getting your butt kicked? Many people think they are not capable of having great success in their lives and their career. Do you? They have not yet found the true answer to their lives' biggest question, which is: "How can I be and how can I have more than what I am and what I have today?" Have you found the answer to this question? However, happiness is a *contributing factor* to being successful and motivated.

SUCCESS MYTHS

SUCCESS MYTH #1

MYTH: "I can't be as successful as other people."

FACT: That is not true! Personal success is measured by how you compare to yourself, not anyone else. In other words, are you living up to your own potential? Are you doing your personal best?

If you are doing your best, then you are among the most successful people on the planet, and you may not even know it! Many of us are not doing our best at anything. Success is achieved at its greatest level when you compare you to yourself and your own capabilities and potential to do your best. Don't be concerned with how successful *others* are compared to you. Be concerned with how successful *you* are compared to yourself!

SUCCESS MYTH #1: "I can't be as successful as other people."

**SUCCESS
MYTH #2:**

"You have to be rich
to start with to
be successful."

SUCCESS MYTH #2

MYTH: "You have to be rich to start with to be
  successful."

FACT: It is not true.

There are an estimated 100,000 new million-
aires created in this country every year, and the
numbers are rising. Most of these new million-
aires are people that take small businesses and
make something more out of them. Most start
with nothing. You don't have to be rich to start
with to be successful. However, you must have
the desire to be rich!

**SUCCESS
MYTH #3:**

This is a frequently
asked question:
"Do I deserve more?"

Remember this, being
successful is not some
mystical dream that
only the rich can
experience. You may
already be successful,
you just don't know it!

SUCCESS MYTH #3

MYTH: I am frequently asked this question:
  "Do I deserve more?"

FACT: Yes, you do deserve more!

I believe that it is at that moment—when you
question your beliefs and make a decision to
accept nothing less than you deserve and will
be happy with—that true change and long-term
unbridled success and motivation can take
place. So, make the decision that you do deserve
more and you're going to get more. Do it right
now! You do deserve more, you will have more,
and you can be better than you are right now.
Believe these thoughts, and internalize them.
Make them part of your existence. Sleep with
them, eat with them, and make them your own.
There's room for you at the top! I promise!

I hope that this section has helped to debunk
some of the success and motivational myths
that you have encountered. Remember, being
successful is not some mystical dream that only
the rich can experience. You may already be
successful; you just don't know it!

CHAPTER 6

SLEEPING FOR SUCCESS!

Iwas always the last one to leave a party! I attribute many past failures of my own to the lack of one simple thing. It's a natural thing that we all do. It's called sleep. For years I wondered why I was always so tired. Do you? I thought that what I suffered from was fatigue due to a hard day at the office. What I really suffered from, and I do mean *suffered* from, was sleep deprivation. A simple lack of sleep can suck the motivation for success right out of you.

I can't tell you how many times in the past I have either stayed up too late or out too long, wasting my time doing other things when I should have been getting some restful sleep. Sleep enables me to wake up with enough mental energy to tackle a tough day of my career and my life. What a difference in my life sleep has made.

Through my research (and, of course, trial and error), I found that sleeping is a requirement for our physical and mental bodies to rebuild themselves. Although I know that researchers do not fully understand exactly why we sleep, they do know that getting some sleep allows us to recharge our batteries. I know. You might be thinking that you will not be making any money while you are asleep, so you won't be getting closer to success. I used to think that way, too.

**Review & Quotes
& for Your Notes**

Sleeping is a requirement for our physical bodies to rebuild themselves.

Lousy work and a loss in productivity will cost you more money than you could ever make during the time that you sleep— I know.

Have you ever noticed that the really successful people around you are never quite as "tired" as you are? Why is that so?

But if you don't get enough sleep, you will not be operating at your best and you risk burning out, like I did many times. Lousy work and a loss in productivity due to sleep deprivation will cost you more money and more in terms of achievement than you could ever make during the time that you sleep.

Have you ever noticed that the really successful people around you are never quite as "tired" as you are? Why is that so?

I believe that allowing yourself to get on a good "sleep schedule" will make a tremendous difference in your life. It has mine.

One answer is that they properly rest themselves with rejuvenating sleep. Think about it. Very seldom do you see the really successful people at your company staying out too late unless they have to. They still go to the parties and have fun; but they leave at a reasonable time, so they can go home to get some sleep. Thus, they get up the next day and can do their best to pursue success.

As a direct result of sleep deprivation even in small quantities, our ability to function at our highest level diminishes with the loss of just a little sleep.

So what do they know that you may not know? They know that it is essential—no, absolutely critical—to be getting their share of restful sleep.

Without proper sleep, everything that we do is more difficult. When I have not had my daily dose of sleep, I find that I have a hard time doing even the most mundane things, things that I can usually tolerate doing. Research shows my theory to be accurate. As a direct result of sleep deprivation—even in small quantities—our ability to function at our highest level diminishes. We can experience things like a lack of concentration, paranoia, advanced levels of psychosis, reduced alertness, and poor decision-making capabilities. Interestingly enough, when we are properly rested we perform better.

I believe that one of the things that ultimately leads to an inability to concentrate, focus, and have a good attitude is the lack of sleep. A lack of sleep is exactly why many of us fail to become successful. My theory is simple. Many of us are so fatigued from staying up too late, watching television, partying, or worrying about what "might happen" that when we try to get out of bed and go to work to become successful, we are brain-dead. We are too tired to do our jobs well enough to become any better than average.

"Research shows that those who average eight hours of sleep are less likely to die due to cancer, heart problems or stroke."
—David S. Bell in *Curing Fatigue: A step by step plan to uncover and eliminate the causes of chronic fatigue*

So, how much sleep do you need? No one knows but you. How much sleep do you need in order for you to wake up feeling refreshed most every day? Whatever the amount is, get that amount of sleep and get it regularly. Here's something that I find interesting: Have you ever noticed how getting too much sleep leaves you feeling like you have had no sleep at all? The secret to utilizing a personal sleep schedule or sleep pattern is to find out how much sleep you need on a daily basis and get that amount consistently.

We experience an inability to concentrate, focus, and have a good attitude due to a lack of sleep. I believe that is exactly why many of us fail to become successful.

Here's how to identify your sleep pattern
All you have to do is to keep a record of how much sleep you get each night. Keep a log of how long you slept and how you felt after each night of sleep. Do this every day for a couple of weeks. Pretty soon, you will find a pattern or a number of hours of sleep that fits your sleep needs. Whether it's seven hours or eight hours and ten minutes does not matter. What matters is that you identify the optimum amount of sleep you need, your "sleep pattern." Once you identify the number of hours and minutes of sleep you need, get that much sleep each day.

As with every success principle in this book, it's not what you do every once in a while that takes you closer to becoming more successful. It's what you do every day.

Things that add to sleep deprivation: Alcohol, medication, emotional/medical conditions, pain, stress, any one of the many sleep disorders, difficulty in breathing, exercise within three hours of bedtime, caffeine, smoking, being overweight, and snoring, just to name a few.

Things that induce good sleep: exercise, a bath, reading, a glass of warm milk, turkey sandwiches.

Things that induce a good night's sleep: Exercise, a hot bath, reading, a glass of warm milk, turkey sandwiches.

The big question—to nap or not to nap?

In many foreign countries napping is a "must do." Napping is actually an integral part of many cultural beliefs. I don't know that many people that have a lifestyle that allows them to nap very often. Most of the people that I know have to work every day. I believe that it's up to you whether you decide to nap or not. If you can get away with it, and it helps you, then nap.

How long should a nap last?

I don't really know. However, when I get the chance to nap, I try to keep the nap to no more than a half hour. If I nap any longer than that, I feel sluggish—almost worse than before I took the nap—and I have difficulty sleeping that night. Again, this question can only be answered by you.

If you nap during the day and have trouble sleeping at night, don't nap!

My thoughts regarding the napping subject are simple. If you nap during the day and have trouble sleeping at night, don't nap. However, if you can get away with napping during the day, and you fall asleep easily at night, go ahead and nap if you want to. Don't forget, you might be missing out on things for a while during your nap, but if it makes you feel better, then by all means nap a bit.

Sleep disorders

During my research on sleeping behaviors, I read a statement that I found very interesting. I cannot remember where I read it, but it basically said that if it takes you more than 30 minutes in bed to fall asleep at night, you are classified as having insomnia. That being the case, I think we all have had a few nights where we could be classified as insomniacs. Whatever. I am no sleep expert but I do know that we gotta have it.

If you think you have a sleep disorder or are having trouble sleeping, see a doctor. Don't wait for the problem to just go away. Enough said?

CHAPTER 7

WE MUST OVERCOME
THE FEAR OF FAILURE

Why are we afraid of failing? How does the fear of failure affect our desire to become successful?

So why are we afraid of failing?

Why is it we spend so much time trying to succeed, but no time preparing ourselves to succeed?

To truly want to succeed, you must want and need to change what and how you think about failure and your fear of it. I believe that those of us who are more successful than others are more successful partly because they have learned to accept failure as part of the game, so they don't give up at the first sign of troubled times.

Failure can easily make us succumb to the pressures of everyday life. It can make us want to quit everything. I felt this way for much of my life prior to learning how to eliminate the fear of failure from my life and career. I feel sad for those of you who feel or have felt the kind of pain and the pressure that fear can put upon you. It is a kind of life-crippling pain that prevents us from simply enjoying life itself.

Does it seem that achieving even small successes are sometimes out of your reach?

We build comfortable and predictable lives around failure.

It's our fear to take action—our reluctance to do something—that keeps us in the same crummy situation all our lives. Many people find a sense of security in failure; they do nothing to change their consequences and wonder why nothing positive seems to happen for them. Since they feel like they are failures, they begin to crave the pity and sympathy of people who don't really care whether they are successful or not; they no longer desire the praise that comes from being successful. Doing nothing simply becomes a way to gain and attract sympathy and attention, attention that should be given to them for being successful, but isn't.

We hope and dream that we are going to be successful, but hoping and dreaming alone are actionless and not enough to propel us toward success.

Do we do nothing because we are just plain lazy? Or are we really expressing a desperate need to succeed at any cost?

Does it seem that achieving even small successes is sometimes out of your reach?

See if you can relate to this: There have been many times in the past when I have delayed doing something because I thought that I needed a little push to help me get going. I feared failing. Maybe I would receive some help from a great person, who would come into my life and teach me how to be the successful person that I really wanted to be. Guess what...that never happened. I had to eliminate my own fear of failure, stop waiting for someone to come along with all of the answers and just go for what I wanted. Yes, I've had help from many people throughout my life, but ultimately it was me that decided to become something more than average, and it was me that stopped being afraid of failing.

Are we just plain lazy, or are we really expressing a desperate need to succeed at anything at all costs?

By doing nothing, we flex our only power muscle.

Doing nothing can give us a sense of real power. By doing nothing we feel like we are

It's the reluctance to do something—to take action—that keeps us in the same crummy situation all of our lives.

really doing something. You know? Rather than doing something and risking a failure, we'll avoid doing anything; we'll say things like: "I do not have to do anything," or "I'm waiting for the big break to come along," or "I don't think I want to do that because I'm too busy." Ultimately, it's not that we don't want to do anything, it's that we are afraid to do something because we might fail. What happens next? The fear of failure becomes a state of mind as well as a way of life.

We build comfortable and predictable lives around failure.

You must decide how much responsibility and risk you are willing to take on.

Now, since it is easier to just do nothing, and since many of us are accustomed to taking little or no chances in order to succeed, we find that the certainty of giving in to a lifetime of mediocrity is easy to live with and comforting. I know; I have given up on achieving success many times. I've wanted to live on an old boat, to coast and have no bills for a while. There have been periods when I have done nothing for months at a time. Quitting can quickly become more comfortable than actually trying to become successful and risking failure in an attempt to succeed. We can then count on becoming marginally successful, but this is really just an extended form of failure.

Quitting is more comfortable than actually pursuing success and risking failure in an attempt to be successful; we can then count on becoming marginally successful, which is just an extended form of failure.

Becoming marginally successful does not count. Marginally successful means mediocre. By becoming marginally successful, we get a little of both failure and success, which ultimately leads to contentment and a false sense of security. We then minimize our self-worth. This habit is as destructive as anything I know.

We get a little of both failure and success, which leads to contentment and a false sense of security. We then minimize our self-worth. This habit is as destructive as anything I know.

What is the result of allowing failure and acceptance of mediocrity to influence our thinking?

We choose the wrong job, the wrong relation-ship, the wrong career, or the wrong place to live. Our decision-making capabilities become inadequate. Our self-esteem becomes low. We lose hope, and a subtle but consistent habit of failing forms in our lives and our careers. We actually guarantee our own failures by doing some of the stupid things that we do. We defeat ourselves before we even have a chance to succeed. Combine that with the fact that you may be the only one who really wants you to succeed, and you begin to understand how hard trying to become successful is for some of us. Many times, the pursuit of success has simply made me miserable, as I'm sure it has for many others.

What happens when we allow the fear of failure to control us?

We manufacture our own little world of "almost successes," you know, marginal successes and little successes that are trivial in the big picture of things and that are far below our capabilities, but that we make believe are great accomplish-ments. By creating a world where we pretend that we are as successful as we really want to be, we become content. Being content with only marginal success proves to be nothing more than an illusion, a distorted view of this truth: the fear of failing is easier to live with than the pain of pursuing success and failing.

As a culture and a society, we have added more fear to the already huge fear of succeeding. Have you ever heard the phrase, "You gotta pay your dues to be successful"? This statement implies that we must go through some kind of suffering in order to become more successful. Knowing how the mind works, one must then believe that

This false feeling of contentment with marginal success proves to be nothing more than an illusion, a distorted view of this truth: the fear of failing is easier to live with than the pain of pursuing success and failing.

Our basic instinct to succeed is weak! Our basic needs of hope, optimism, and love are not being met. We have been conditioned to accept far less than actual success.

it becomes easy for us to associate suffering and pain to success, which is wrong. Although there can be much pain and suffering in the pursuit of success, it does not have to be that way.

Let's talk about discrimination a minute. Within the ranks of our culture, there is as much or more success discrimination (between the successful and the unsuccessful) as there is minority discrimination. We harshly discriminate against those of us that fail. Those that are successful get all of the glory, while those that are seemingly not successful get passed by and pushed around.

Fear has been built in to our personalities.

Overall, our basic instinct to succeed is weak! Many of our basic needs of hope, optimism, and love are not being met. Many of us have been conditioned to accept far less than what we deserve. We've been beaten up by failure so many times that we just simply take whatever comes at us. We've also become conditioned to be content or complacent, and it has become acceptable for some of us to just give up. Heck, our society even condones it! What do you think welfare is? It's an admission from our government and other extremists that plague this country that says it is OK to do nothing—it's OK to be unsuccessful. Well, it's not OK!

What happens when you eliminate the fear of failing?

You have the freedom to fail, then succeed. Many of the world's most successful people failed miserably time after time, only to learn from their failures and move on to become extremely successful. They learned how not to be afraid of failing. Learning how to deal with failure successfully is the key to making failure

In the pursuit of success, we easily succumb to the pressures of everyday life. It is a kind of life-crippling pain that prevents us from simply enjoying life itself.

If and when you begin to truly believe that you can eliminate the fear of taking action and succeeding, you will begin to accept the way that things are.

For you are destined to be successful. Anything else is a futile way of living.

What happens when you get rid of the fear of failing?

pay off for you. Here's how to deal with failure successfully:

1. You must accept ultimate responsibility for all of your failures.

2. Believe that it is OK to fail; but only if you learn from the failure, and it inspires you to continue your pursuit of success.

3. Accept the fact that no matter what you do, no matter how perfect that you want to be, you will still fail at things from time to time.

If you are going to fail, fail really big!

Fail in a way that will gain you the attention, admiration, and the sympathy of others, and use it to your advantage. Make a positive out of a negative. As an example, look at former President Richard Nixon's record of failure. His career was so loaded with failures that it caused him to resign from office. Yet almost every failure that he had experienced brought him closer and closer to the Presidency, because he knew how to fail and how to capitalize on a failure. He actually *failed* his way to the top and then back down to the bottom.

Occasional failures can help you!

Do you learn from OCCASIONAL failures? What can be good about failing?

Michael Korda, author of *Success*, wrote: "Projects fail, plans fail, companies fail—you need not." A successful life, the pursuit of happiness, and true fulfillment both in our lives and our careers are results of constantly learning from our failures and gaining some wisdom from each failure. We can then try not to make the same mistake again. Common sense tells us not to do stupid things twice.

> Learning how to deal with failure successfully is the key to making failure pay off.

> Do you learn from OCCASIONAL failures? What can be good about failing?

> An OCCASIONAL failure is an inherent and consistent part of life.

An OCCASIONAL failure can teach you more than a success.

An OCCASIONAL failure can teach you more than success and is an inherent and consistent part of life.

View an occasional failure as a learning experience. This makes failing a little easier to live with. Failing teaches us respect for success and allows us to accept responsibility—literally forcing us to become more humble.

Remember these tips when dealing with failures in your life and your career:

1. Failure is part of the game.

2. Give yourself a break! You don't have to "make it big" this instant. Succeeding takes a little time and preparation.

3. Commit yourself to your dreams and your goals 110%. Don't do anything halfway or you're destined to fail from the beginning.

4. Learn what you can from each failure and move on. Don't dwell on the crummy stuff!

5. Prepare yourself to be successful with a plan that will help you minimize your failures.

If and when you begin to truly believe that you can eliminate the fear of failing from your life and your career, you will begin to accept the way that things are. You will be more motivated to learn how to beat—and work within—a system that is designed for many of us to fail. You can then truly begin a process of accepting life on no other terms but your own. Fear is not an option. For you are destined to be successful. Anything else is a futile way of thinking and living.

CHAPTER 8

INTUITIVE CONSCIOUSNESS

WORK • FUN • RELATIONSHIPS • SELF • ENERGY

Have you ever met someone and immediately felt that you did not like that person? Have you ever felt like some of the decisions that you make go against your best judgment? Have you ever gotten advice from someone and felt that the advice was wrong, but you did what they advised you to do anyway?

Review & Quotes & for Your Notes

After years of trying everything to be successful, I looked more closely at what I had done that had not brought me nearer to my dreams and goals (some insight time) and found that I was simply not thinking properly; I was not acting upon my clearest thoughts and perceptions— my intuitions. I was thinking neither intuitively nor consciously. Consequently, I made far more mistakes than I should have. That changed when I developed a simple thinking process that I call "Intuitive Consciousness."

Have you ever had an idea to start a business, and you just *felt* like it would make it? That feeling is an intuitive thought. Thinking about doing it would be a conscious thought. Doing it would be an "Intuitive Consciousness" thought and decision.

Before I define Intuitive Consciousness, let's first find out exactly what the definition of "intuit" and "conscious" are. According to *The Random House Dictionary*, "intuit" is defined as:

1. direct perception of the truth or fact, independent of any reasoning process.

2. a keen and quick insight.

"Conscious" is defined as:

1. knowing one's own existence, surroundings, etc.

2. having the mental faculties fully active.

3. known to oneself: conscious guilt.

4. deliberate or intentional.

So, what is "INTUITIVE CONSCIOUSNESS"?

Intuitive consciousness is a method of thinking. It's a thought process. It requires us to think more intuitively and consciously with regards to what and how we do, what it is that we do. It's a process that combines:

1. our intuitions—the things that we feel are right, and

2. our conscious or rational state of mind.

Intuitive consciousness is the combination of listening to intuitions, making conscious decisions, and balancing them between the things that require our attention. These are our work, fun, relationships, ourselves, and our energies.

Intuitive consciousness simply requires that we listen to our intuitions, our feelings regarding what our thoughts and emotions tell us, and then consciously think about what the results of our actions will be. Then we decide, based upon our intuitive feelings and our conscious or rational thoughts, whether to do or not to do

INTUITIVE CONSCIOUSNESS is a simple process. It simply requires that we intuitively listen to what our thoughts, feelings, and emotions are telling us and consciously think about what the results of our actions will be, then make our decisions based upon our intuitive feelings.

things that may take us closer to our dreams and goals.

Why don't we listen to our intuitions and our conscious more often?

I have several theories to explain why this happens, one of which is the fact that many of us fear making our own decisions. Instead of listening to our intuitions and our feelings, we disregard them and take the advice of others. This turns out to be a mistake more times than not. Another theory is that some of us are so fed up with trying to become successful that we accept mediocrity, avoiding our intuitions as a way of not taking chances. It becomes more comfortable to ignore our intuitions and do whatever.

You see, it's when we do not listen intuitively and consciously to what our minds, our spirits, and our bodies are telling us that depression, anxiety, bad decisions, failures, and guilt can overcome us. An example is when our spirit for work is telling us that our energies are drained, but we double our work efforts in an attempt to silence what we hear from our intuitions; we are not listening intuitively or consciously to what's being said. At this point, we are in our most vulnerable state; we make our biggest mistakes and worst decisions right here.

INTUITIVE CONSCIOUSNESS is a process that requires us to:

1. Consciously identify what we intuitively feel are the most important aspects of a successful and quality way of life for us as individuals.

2. Prioritize each of these intuitions and conscious decisions every day, based upon how much time of our life they consume.

3. Put what we feel are the most important aspects of a successful way of life into proper perspective, and prioritize them.

When we can intuitively and consciously focus our attention on what I believe are the five most important of these aspects, we can seriously enhance the quality of our lives and the lives of the people around us. It is essentially the process of intuitively and consciously being aware of what happens to us and what we do to make things happen to us.

The five aspects of Intuitive Consciousness are: WORK, FUN, RELATIONSHIPS, OURSELVES, and OUR FOUR ENERGIES.

THE FIVE ASPECTS OF INTUITIVE CONSCIOUSNESS

The five areas that I have personally identified follow, but please keep in mind that I have listed them in no particular order. I feel that each of them is equally vital to a successful way of life. You may identify five completely different aspects; this strategy is subject to interpretation.

1. **WORK**

2. **FUN**

3. **RELATIONSHIPS**

4. **OURSELVES**

5. **OUR ENERGIES**

These are what I believe to be the most important aspects of an "intuitive consciousness" approach to prioritizing our thoughts. If you agree with the five aspects that I have identified, that's great. Learn from them and expand upon them. If you don't agree with them, indulge me for a bit. Read on and formulate your own interpretation of intuitive consciousness. Then, make a decision to intuitively and consciously put each of the areas that you identify as the most important things in your life into perspec-

We are not intuitively and consciously thinking and living; many of us only "exist" in a world that influences our every thought, if we do not influence these thoughts for ourselves.

tive. Without this level of intuitive planning and conscious awareness, we are simply "winging it" in our lives and in our careers. We are not Intuitively and Consciously living life. I believe that many of us only "exist" in a world that influences our every thought, if we do not influence these thoughts for ourselves.

If we have not planned, identified, and prioritized what we intuitively and consciously feel is important to us, how can we really expect to be fulfilled in life or achieve a higher level of success?

Intuitive Consciousness and Our Work

Does working 9–5 feel like you are doing 5–10?

Think about this a minute: If you are 30 years old and work a 9–5 day, and you plan to retire a little early, say when you're 60 instead of 65, guess how many hours you will have worked? 60,000 hours! Don't forget to live life a little bit. There is more to life than work!

My work today is only a portion of my life. A portion that I now enjoy and choose to do for myself. It is an extension of who I really am. I choose my work not because my family or my spouse thinks I should, but because *I* think I should; because it makes me feel good.

Why do you do your work?

I had to change my perception of my work so I could think more intuitively and search for some fulfillment in it. Changing our perception—how we perceive our work—is how we add power and fulfillment to our lives regarding our work, even if it is among the most mundane of all work.

We are successful in our work when we can best get a sense of fulfillment and joy, when our work

How can we really expect to be fulfilled in life or achieve a higher level of success if we have not planned, identified, and prioritized what we intuitively feel is important to us?

Does working 9–5 feel like you are doing 5–10?

There is more to life than work.

How do you perceive your work?

is only an extension of who we are and what we do. For example, I am a sales trainer, author, and motivational speaker. It gives me great joy to teach what I have learned and to share it with others. Knowing that I have helped another person gives me a sense of fulfillment, and that sense of fulfillment allows me to intuitively and consciously prioritize my work with my life. I still do have to *practice* intuitive consciousness, for if I do not, I find that my work will entrap me; it will confuse me with the joy from the work that I pursue with passion, thus masking the joy and passion that I now seek in my life through fun, relationships, myself, and my energies.

> We are successful in our work when we can best get a sense of fulfillment and joy, when our work is only an extension of who we are and what we do.

Successful people view their work as an art. Not that they consider themselves great artists, but they see their work as "what they do, what they love to do," and they receive a sense of pride and fulfillment from their work. As Dick Richards wrote in his book, *Artful Work*: "All work is part art, part science." I believe that is true. He continued to write: "An Artist attempts to create a balance among the joy of work, pride in the product, and a satisfying livelihood."

> I have found that the truly successful people in this world view their work as an art.

Many of us have simply devalued our work. Do you value your work as an art?

> Do you value your work as an art?

Is your work ever done? Can you leave your work at the office? When you come home do you think of nothing but your work? Are you doing work that you receive joy and fulfillment from? Do you like your work?

> Is your work ever done? Can you leave your work at the office, or do you think of nothing but work when you come home? Are you doing work that you receive joy and fulfillment from?

Your work should not make you miserable!

If, as I have in the past, you don't like your work or your life, you build a kind of dissatisfaction that can be devastating to you and everyone around you. As a result, you will find that success is as far away from you as it will ever be. I'm not saying quit your job tomorrow if you hate it, but don't do work that you hate for any longer than you have to. By performing a job or work that you hate, you violate the basic laws of success and successful living—which are to enjoy your work and to enjoy your life.

If you don't like what you are doing, do something else! Don't do it for the money or for the power that you can receive from the job. Do your work for a feeling of satisfaction and fulfillment. When you do, you will find that success will pursue you, instead of you pursuing success. Our dissatisfied feelings regarding work simply come from doing work that we do not enjoy. Unhappiness at work seems to bring about a reduction of consciousness and a decrease in the vitality of simply living. After all, we spend the majority of our lives working.

Why do we do work that we do not enjoy?

Think about this a minute: Unless you are independently wealthy and do not have to work, you'll probably have to spend around 70% of your time working. For money? Fame? Notoriety? For recognition? For what? Find a way to make your work fun, fulfilling, and enjoyable!

Let's reexamine our reasons for working. I believe most of us do work that we don't like for three reasons.

Reason #1: Money

Many of us work for a steady paycheck and the false sense of security that it provides. I'm not telling you not to work for money; I'm merely saying that money is not the only reason to go to work. I like to be paid for my work,

Do you like your work?

If, as I did, you don't like your work or your life, you build a kind of dissatisfaction that can be devastating to you and everyone around you. At this point, you will find that success is as far away from you as it will ever be.

Don't do it for money or the power that you can receive; do your work for a feeling of satisfaction and fulfillment.

Why do we do work that we do not enjoy?

Think about this a minute. Unless you are independently wealthy and do not have to work, you'll probably have to spend around 70% of your time working. For money? Fame? Notoriety? For recognition? For what?

Many of us work for a steady paycheck and for the false sense of security it provides, rather than for our need for fulfillment.

It's unfortunate that many of us find it difficult or impossible to "start over" and do what we really enjoy because we have accumulated too much debt doing the things that we don't like doing. When you think about it, that seems really stupid of us, doesn't it?

we all do, but I am equally fulfilled by the work that I do and the people that I help. Those feelings allow me to continue my work, no matter what the payoff is in terms of dollars.

How can we fix the problem?

Identify what it is that you really want to do. If you have to, start small. Try doing what you want to do as a hobby and build on it from there. That is how I started my company. This approach is realistic; it's rational. However, quitting a job that is stressing you out and moving to the beach is not rational in most cases. I should know; I did it.

Reason #2

The question we need to ask ourselves is not: "What would I do if I could just start over?" The question we need to ask is: "What will I do with the time I have left on the planet when I start over?"

We are afraid of starting over for fear of failing. We do not have enough faith in our ability to make a living doing what we enjoy doing. The question we need to ask ourselves is not: "What would I do if I could just start over?" The question we need to ask ourselves is: "What will I do with the time I have left on the planet when I start over?"

Reason #3

We've made a mistake and buried ourselves in debt.

It's unfortunate that many of us find it difficult or impossible to "start over" and do what we really enjoy for work because we have accumulated too much debt doing the things that we don't enjoy. When you think about, that seems really stupid of us, doesn't it?

I have been faced with overcoming all three of the previous obstacles and more. When I started my company, I had little finances in reserve to draw from. However, through my persistence and the help of a good friend, I was able to start small and find the capital needed in order to get started. That fixed problem #1.

Next, I knew that I could provide other people with training that would benefit them, but I seriously questioned my faith in my own ability to be a trainer and speaker, and to make a living doing it. Many times, in the beginning, I lost faith in myself. I am thankful, however, that my friends, family, and clients never lost their faith in me. You know what? After receiving the encouragement of my friends and family, the positive comments from my clients, and the paycheck for my first real seminar/workshop, it soon became evident to me that I indeed had something to offer to others; my faith in myself was quickly renewed. That fixed problem #2.

Finally, I knew that I was already deep in debt when I started. I figured what the heck! I might as well go all the way! That fixed problem #3, and I was off and running. I've always said, if I'm ever going to go down hard, I'm going down in style. First class all the way down! I'll hit every ATM from Florida to France.

Additionally, there was my fear of what other people would say or think about my new career path. However, I quickly realized that I did not care what anyone but me thought or said about me. At that moment—I still remember it— I realized that I had become more successful than ever before. I had won the biggest battle, I think, of my entire life. That changed my way of life forever. I defeated my own fear of trying. I had finally made a decision to do what I wanted to do because I enjoyed doing it, and it made me feel good. I'd taken my fate out of the hands of others and placed it into my own, and it felt great. Win, lose, or draw, big time or little time, success or failure, I decided to risk everything for my dream of being a trainer and speaker. No longer did I need the approval of others; I only needed my own. That feels great to this day. I think these words illustrate the situation well: "Commit yourself to a dream.... Nobody who tries to do something in life is a complete failure. Why? Because he can rest assured that he has defeated life's most important battle. He defeated the fear of trying" (Robert H. Schuller). Smart guy, don't you think?

I believe that our work is more satisfying and fulfilling when, through a process of intuitive consciousness, we make our work an artistic expression of who we really are. Our perception of our work then becomes much more than simple work; it becomes a process of mastering the artistry behind our work. What do I mean by artistic, or artistry? In his book *Artful Work,* author Dick Richards describes it as follows: "We are artful about our work when we use the materials of the MOMENT in an act of CENTERING that, assisted by COMMITMENT to mastery of a medium, brings concreteness to a VISION; bringing all four forms of human energy...Physical, Intellectual, Emotional, and Spiritual, To The Moment." I say, right on Dick!

Intuitive Consciousness and Fun!

What do you do that you consider really fun?

What do you do that you consider fun? Do you have a hobby?

Do you have a hobby?

I simply believe that having fun is what successful living is all about. One of the reasons we work is to make enough money to be able to afford to have fun, isn't it? I don't think we are here to exist in a stressed-out environment where we are depressed and always wanting more. I am convinced that life is supposed to be fun. Like financial rewards for being successful, having fun in our lives and our work is a consequence—a reward for the successful completion of good habits.

Fun is what rejuvenates our spirit to work hard. It recharges our batteries. Fun is how we relieve the mind and the body of stress and anxiety. Without fun, life can truly be miserable. For years I had very little fun. So, what changed for me? I began to listen intuitively and consciously to what my mind and my body said to me about having fun; I *learned* how to have fun.

When was the last time that you had fun?

When was the last time that you had fun?

I mean *real* fun! Let me qualify this question. Don't confuse fun with work; they are not the same. When was the last time that you did something that was fun, not because you were good at it, but because it was fun? You know, the kind of fun that sets your mind at ease when you are done. The kind that makes you anticipate doing it again. So, when was the last time you really had some fun?

There are many of us who simply don't have enough fun. We work too much, never understanding that if we'd just intuitively listen to what our minds and our bodies are telling us, we'd have more fun. This would in turn make us even more productive at our work, thus allowing us to succeed faster. I know for a fact that after a short while of not having fun, our performance actually gets worse. It makes sense. The harder we work, the less that we play and have fun, the more depressed and anxious we feel—right? Well, that being the case, it would also make sense to relieve our stress and anxiety by taking a break from everything else and having some regular fun, right?

It is easy to trick ourselves into thinking we're having fun. Sometimes, in reality, we are really working. Let me give you an example.

I had this motorcycle. It was a 750 Kawasaki Ninja, and it was really fast. I loved riding it, because it helped to relieve the stress of the day. Riding it was pure fun. The feeling of acceleration, the feeling of the road and the wind seemed to calm me and give me some peace of mind. A short ride would often give me some time to forget about everything that was on my mind except the experience of the ride. Occasionally, I have been known to top over 160 mph. It was fun! Wrong, but fun. (Nobody is perfect.)

Anyway, I like to go fast when I ride, obviously. However, going fast quickly became less like fun and more like work. You have to be constantly aware of everything around you. It would be bad to hit something, you know. It takes a lot more concentration and thought to handle the machine when it is ridden fast. One day, when I went for a ride to see my old friend Steve, I realized this was happening to me. The trip began as a pleasant, sort of lazy ride that allowed me to enjoy the feel of simply riding the machine and enjoying the scenery. But I soon got bored. Right about the time the stress and anxiety of the past few days went away, I began to race against time and see how fast I could make it to his place. At that point, the ride became more like work and, consequently, less enjoyable in the end.

Do you feel guilty when you're having fun because you are not working? You shouldn't!

You should feel more guilty for denying yourself some fun. Don't you deserve to have fun and enjoy life? I think you do! Don't feel guilty for leaving your work and having some fun. You are supposed to have fun.

Do you feel guilty when you're having fun because you are not working? You shouldn't!

Why do we feel guilty when we're having fun?

Do you feel guilty when you're not working and having some fun? Maybe it's because the moment you realize that you do need to have some fun, you also realize that you have wasted most of the time that you allocated to do your work. Consequently, you may feel guilty because you did not get your work done. Remedy this by learning how to utilize your energy, control your focus, and plan your workday properly as described in this book.

Do you feel like if you are not working, you won't reach your goals and make as much money?

The fact is, if you don't take some time out to have fun, you risk burning out.

This is a common misconception. It's an obsession for work rather than fun that many of us suffer from today. The fact is, if you don't take some time out to have fun, you risk burning out. Then where will you be? You will have put a double whammy on yourself by not taking the time to have fun.

So, how do we balance the two, work and fun?

So, how do we balance the two, work and fun?

By using the process that I described earlier: "Intuitive Consciousness." Using I.C., we can learn how to detect when we are in need of fun and thus prevent much of the depression and anxiety that can accompany the pursuit of success.

I have heard many excuses for not having fun from many people. What are yours?

No More Excuses!

I have heard many excuses for not having fun. What are yours? Let's look more closely at some excuses that irritate me the most. I have been guilty of using these myself. "I don't have enough time to have fun." "I can't afford to have fun." "I'm not finished with my work yet."

Now let's debunk them.

Excuse #1: Not enough time? What do you mean you don't have enough time? Making this excuse only gives us a reason to stay at work. We all have an equal amount of time each day to have fun and to do our work. Those of us who are successful have found a way to balance the two. If you think that you truly don't have enough time to have fun, maybe you should look at how you utilize your time and decide if you are using it effectively. You might need a time-management course.

Are you using your time effectively? Are you wasting your time?

Excuse #2: "I can't afford to have any fun." Guess what? None of us unless we are making the big bucks or at least are independently wealthy can actually afford to have fun. This is a false rationalization of the issue. My point here is not whether any of us can afford to have fun; my point is that none of us can afford *not* to have fun. Don't let the lack of money stand in the way of enjoying life and having fun. Don't you think that is sort of backwards? We work to have the money to afford to have fun, but we don't end up spending it on having fun. That's nuts!

Excuse #3: "I'm not finished with my work yet." Guess what? Again, if you are not independently wealthy, if you do not own your own company or make enough bucks to hire someone else and delegate all of your work to them, you'll probably work for someone else throughout your entire

Are you using your time effectively? Are you wasting your time?

We work to have the money to afford to have fun, but we don't end up spending it on having fun. That's nuts!

career. That being the case, your work will never be "finished." You may never catch up on all the work that you have to do. All you can do is do as much quality work as you can. Think about it. Being employed by someone else essentially means that your work is never going to be done. There will always be a project. There will always be someone asking you why you are taking time off. There will always be something, some reason or excuse, why you can't go have fun.

What to do next?

Well, I am no time management expert, but I do know what worked for me. First, I had to learn how to listen to my intuitions. Then I decided to plan some time every other day simply to have fun. The difference that this one little thing made in my life is incredible. I feel better. I work and concentrate better. I sleep better. My mood swings are much more controllable. My relationships with others have improved. My desire to actually work and work well has increased. All of this is a result of adding some fun to my life. Now, I like to have fun so much that sometimes I forget that I have to work, which is a good thing.

These excuses are nonsense!

They are simple excuses that we make to keep us thinking that we are happy doing other stuff like work when we are not happy at all. Excuses hold you back! The price for success that you may be paying by not having some regular fun is not worth unhappiness. I like to rationalize the issue like this: When I am old and gray and sitting in a diaper in some nursing home or whatever (assuming I live that long), the only things that I will want to reflect on are the memories of the fun I had throughout my life and the people I had fun with. I do not want

> Think about it. Being employed by someone else means that our work is never done.

to be sitting there in a dirty diaper waiting for somebody to clean me up, thinking: "I wish I'd done more; I wish I'd had more fun." Memories of the fun that we have had are memories that we cannot afford to be without. So go have some fun!

What's your excuse for not putting this book down right now and having some fun?

Intuitive Consciousness and Relationships

If you are successful, you can become a threat to everyone around you!

Find the Right Person to Help You Succeed!

Success without someone to share it with spells loneliness. But your friends, your spouse, and your family really want you to be successful, don't they? NOT! They may want you to fail. Let's find out why.

Why would other people like to see you fail? Because they can control you if you are a failure, or if you are only marginally successful like them. Relationships and success can be tough. You see, if you are only marginally successful, other people can ride your coat tails, control you, and be better than you. That makes them feel great and you feel like a failure. If you are only marginally successful, it's not uncommon to find out that other people do want and even need to be around you. It's when you threaten to outgrow them that the trouble begins. Here's what typically happens next. It happened to me after I left college; I lost touch with my bodybuilding, football-playing buddies. It's simple, I changed and became more successful at that time than they were. I got a job and stopped interacting with them;

What's your excuse for not putting this book down right now and having some fun?

when that happened, the relationship between us changed. Now, if you are one of the old buddies and you know that this change is coming, what do you do?

Much of what traditionally happens is one of two things. Either a conspiracy to sabotage the other person's success begins, or the successful person forgets his or her friends and moves on, maybe thinking that he doesn't need those friends anymore. What happens is the "successful" person ends up lonely, and the other people end up moving on and making new friends. This is exactly what happened to me. I became a threat to some of my old friends with my newfound success. They became less important to me than my career. While they were still having fun and taking on little or no responsibility for anything, I was out there making sales calls every day, trying to build a career and make a living. I still wish that I had those friends around me today. Losing my friends was yet another mistake I made in pursuit of success. A lack of commitment, a selfish lack of dedication, and a poor sense of security can be attributed to this.

You become a threat to those around you when you become successful! Other people can actually hold you back from achieving success. They subtley do things to keep you held down or held back. Most of these things are not really done on purpose; they are performed on more of a subconscious level and are due to their simple fear of losing you and their jealousy.

What really happens is that your success threatens the comfort of everyone around you. It scares the heck out of them; you scare the heck out of them. You become a tremendous

Your friends, your spouse, and your family really want you to be successful, don't they?

Why would others like to see you fail?

Have you ever noticed how other people will stand in line to grab the glory of a particular success with you, or even take credit for helping you when they have done nothing to actually help you?

You become a threat to those around you when you become successful.

threat to others. You threaten to outdo them, outearn them, and outgrow them. Without a truly humble attitude, you may eventually leave them behind and possibly lose your friends or family forever. You see, it is up to you to give them a feeling of comfort. They need to know that no matter how successful you become, you will not forget them. Only the most intuitive and successful people in the world—people who have mastered themselves, their relationships, and their communications—can relieve the pressure of being a threat to others. They find a way; they make it a goal to enlist their friends and families to help them become more successful, rather than pushing them away. How will you deal with other people's feelings of your success?

How will you deal with other people's feelings of your success?

If the other people in your life really wanted you to be successful, would they encourage you to do some of the stupid things that they encourage you to do?

If the other people in your life really wanted you to be successful, would they encourage you to do some of those stupid things that they encourage you to do?

Here are some examples: If your friends and family really wanted you to be successful, would they turn their heads as you cheat on your wife, watch you drink too much and drive home drunk, call your boss so you and your friends can skip out on work to play golf, or maybe watch you eat a bag of cookies when you are on a diet? Of this I am certain. Few of the "friends" that you will encounter in life will really take the time to give a hoot about you. Ultimately, they can suck the will to succeed out of you, until you become content with being average or just above average—just like them. In other words, it makes a difference who you choose to call your friend. You see, if the other people in your life really wanted you to be successful, they would share in your success and try to do nothing to get in your way.

Recruit Them!

I've found through experience that one of our biggest goals must be to make the other people in our lives want us to be successful as badly as we want to be successful.

It is up to you to create an ideal perception of yourself for the people close to you to share and believe regarding you and your success. If everyone thinks of you as successful, they help to confirm your own beliefs. This is how you get and give power from relationships in life. Whatever you do, don't ever let them hear you complain or ask for sympathy. This will weaken your position as a successful person, in your mind and theirs.

Imagine the commitment in terms of unselfishness, love, dedication, understanding, support, motivation, and financial responsibility it must take from friends and family for a person trying to become an Olympic athlete. The training schedule, diet, lack of time with loved ones, restrictions, and traveling schedule alone must put a tremendous strain on relationships. Yet, in Atlanta in 1996, there were thousands of these special athletes from around the world with loved ones and friends, who were there attempting to help them bring home the gold. What would you have been able to accomplish to date, if you could have had that kind of dedication to your success from the people in your life?

Three things that you will continually read about in this book will help you succeed in recruiting your friends and family. I believe

Only the most intuitive and successful people in the world—people who have mastered themselves, relationships, and communications—can relieve the pressure of being a threat to others.

Your goal must be to make the other people in your life want you to be successful as badly as *you* want to be successful.

What would you have been able to accomplish if you could have had that kind of dedication to your success from the people in your life?

these three words are the keys to mastering life and harnessing true success. They are:

1: Relationships

2: Communications

3: Yourself

Success Can Change a Relationship

Jealousy. Really a bad thing in a relationship. I know from experience. Marriages can withstand failures. Most of them are built around failures. But, for the following reasons—and those I have already mentioned—few can withstand real success.

Statistically, marriages that begin during the early stages of success for one or both of the individuals have a better long-term success rate than marriages that have to deal with a partner who suddenly becomes successful. If the relationship is strong going in, it has a good chance of surviving success. If it is weak going in, a breakup is likely to occur.

For the less successful spouse in the relationship, it is easier to contend with failures because small continuous failures are allowable. These failures feed off of sympathy from the other partner. Codependency, false love, hope, money, and greed are the results of poor relationships. These things keep two people bound together by necessity and fear, not by love.

If you agree with me so far, then this will make sense to you. If you are mastering the art of communications, relationships, and yourself, then you should not end up in a divorce over sudden success. Rather, you will use the success to improve your relationship and both of your lives.

Margin notes:

Three words are the keys to mastering life and harnessing true success: 1. Relationships, 2. Communications, and 3. Yourself.

Marriages can withstand failures; hell, most of them are built around failures. But few can withstand real success.

Failures feed off of sympathy from the other partner. Codependency, false love, hope, money and greed are the results. These things keep two people bound together by necessity, not by love.

We all know that changing even little things can be scary. So our mates, loved ones, and friends avoid change. They'll often make you avoid change too, which ultimately leads to your failure and their continued control over you. People feel safe in a world of marginal success, but when real success hits, usually no one is ready for it. This is only the beginning of events that could lead to a breakup of friendships and marriages. Don't allow yourself to be caught up in relationships that consist of roles that imply "success free" love, the kind of partners that say: "I don't care what you do or how much money you have; I will still love you just the same." The result is that you settle for a lack of commitment, dedication, understanding, or caring. What you need to hear from your partner or spouse is: "I don't care how much money you have or how successful you become; I just want to be a part of your life and help you to become happier."

Success is meaningless without someone to share it with.

Success is meaningless without someone to share it with.

No matter how successful or rich we may become, we have to remember that we are creatures of nature; and our nature is to have someone to share both our successes and our failures with.

There are many people who have lost the only person they ever really loved to success. Some losses are justifiable and some are not. If we intuitively and consciously make an effort to include our loved ones, there will surely be greater payoffs.

First, you need to understand intuitively and consciously that success will try to separate you from everything that you have and love but success itself. Second, you must take the necessary steps to prevent success from doing so by spending adequate time cultivating healthy relationships. They are the keys to maintaining and building relationships. In other words, do not get obsessed with success. Rather, get obsessed with the fulfillment and the rewards of healthy relationships, for which you have recruited the help and care that you need.

Find the right person to help you succeed.

Find the right person to help you succeed.

One of the hardest lessons that I have ever learned is that even I need help from others in order to succeed. It is very difficult to succeed at much of anything alone. You must find someone. The right person will stand by you and support you whether you succeed or fail.

Finding the right person to help me succeed throughout my endeavors has been one of the toughest things I have ever done, mostly because I have been a complete jerk for most of my life. I've realized through experience that much of my success depends on my own ability to create relationships with people that can and will help me succeed. I have learned how to recruit people, instead of pushing them away with a narcissistic attitude.

Intuitive Consciousness and Ourselves!

The greatest conflict to overcome is within ourselves!

The greatest conflict that we must face is within ourselves.

One of the biggest obstacles I have had to overcome in order to become more successful was a conflict that existed inside of me. It was not a conflict over money or power. Rather, it was a conflict between "the many *me*'s that I am." The *me*'s that exist in each of us.

According to psychologists, we generally spend about 97% of our time thinking of nothing but ourselves. That being the case, I must have spent around 99% of my time thinking about myself, which may have led to the many ignorant things that I've done.

According to psychologists, we generally spend about 97% of our time thinking of nothing but ourselves.

Only after finding out more about the real me and the "*me*'s that I am," did I fully understand who I really was and what I really wanted to be and do with my life. For years, my life was completely out of control. Is yours?

Yes, there were many nights that I cried myself to sleep because I was so miserable with the way that I felt about myself and the fact that I had not become successful despite all of the things that I'd tried. It hurts me to this day to think of the pain that I put my wife and family through. I am now trying to make up for it every day. Funny, I realize that I was successful all along. I just did not know it.

Looking back as I write this, I understand how truly fortunate I was to have had the resources, money, friends, and family to be able to take the necessary time to refocus my life on what I believed to be important. I thanked each one of them, again, right after writing this.

Yes. The entire process of getting to know the real me was a painful yet joyful experience, and going through it was one of the most difficult trials that I have ever encountered. But, it was the best thing that I have ever done.

As I began discovering the real me, I quickly realized that I desperately needed professional help to sort through the years of miserable existence that I called my life and my career. I needed to get some optimism back in my life. What my counselor and I found together was not all that bad; in fact, it was actually pretty good.

My counselor? I will keep his name anonymous but I will describe him as a realistic man with strong values, and morals that far exceeded my expectations. He is a man who has been through some painful experiences and hard times in his own life.

We learned to have a great deal of respect for one another and through our discussions he taught me how to respect myself. You see, one of the things that I lost during the pursuit of success was respect for myself, because I'd not become as successful as I believed I should be. He also helped me find the good things about myself. I knew they existed but was afraid to show them to anyone. I learned to deal with my past failures and clear my conscience of things that I've done, things that were harmful to myself and others and were continually eating away at me—and more. I'm a nice person, but my obsession to become successful made me do some stupid things.

Through his process of leading me to my own conclusions, not dictating to me his thoughts or his way of life, thus influencing my decisions, we were able to find the real me. This gave me a second chance to continue on with a clear conscience, a greater understanding of who and what I really was, and a renewed sense of self-worth and self-esteem. The truth? He helped save my life, and for that I thank him. I will never forget him. I am still learning how to live successfully and apply the strategies in this book. I now understand that it is a never ending learning process—this thing called life and the pursuit of success. Only after completing this introspective and painful process am I now able to make decisions and commitments to improve my quality of life every day. I am living with a better balance between the many *me*'s that I am.

The Me's That I Am and
The Seven Self-concepts

After going through many miserable and failed attempts at success the first time around, I now realize that the most insurmountable conflict for me was not with everyone else, as I had thought for so long. It was a combination of conflicts between them and my concepts of myself. In other words, I was setting myself up to fail; and fail I did, due to a false sense of who and what I was and what I wanted from my life and my career. I gave people reasons not to like me. I gave people too many reasons to call me a jerk, among other things. The me I really am was getting beaten by the me that I wish I were and the other *me's* that exist in me.

What do you really want out of life? What conflicts exist inside you?

Simply put, the "narcissistic me" had adopted some pretty bad habits, ones that break all of the basic laws of being successful. For many years, I guess I didn't have the courage to be the *me* that I really wanted to be. Do you have the courage to be the *you* that you really want to be?

Generally, I am a very emotional, confident, and giving person but I was acting and performing like a narcissistic, greedy, and uncaring person. According to a publication written by Robert D. Weber entitled *The Self Concept and Success,* there are seven self-concepts each of us shares in ourselves. Let's explore them together.

What do you really want out of life? What conflict exists inside the many me's that you are?

I didn't have the courage to be the *me* that I really wanted to be. Do you?

The seven Self-concepts

1. The me I think I am

2. The me I wish I were

3. The me I really am

4. The me I try to project

5. The me others perceive

6. The me I used to be

7. The me others try to
make me

The Seven Self-concepts

1. The me I think I am

2. The me I wish I were

3. The me I really am

4. The me I try to project

5. The me others perceive

6. The me I used to be

7. The me others try to make me

Do you recognize any of the seven *me*'s within you?

Do you recognize any of
the seven Self-concepts or
me's within you?

Another thing that helped me was putting each of the seven *me*'s into a more healthy perspective. Now, many things mean a great deal more to me than I had previously thought. I spent too much time dreaming about the me that I wish I were and wishing that I was someone else, when I should have been focusing my energy on improving the me that I really am. Do you?

The seven *me*'s I am. How will you relate to them?

1. The me I think I am

Each of us has a "me I think I am." This self-concept is the 'what' and 'who' you think that you are. Who are you?

1. The me I think I am

Who do you think
you are?

Do you think that you are a good person, or do you think negatively about yourself? If you are happy with the real you, you probably think positively about yourself, and that is good. If you think negatively about yourself, then your concept of yourself, "the me you think you are," needs some work. Building up your self-esteem and self-worth is a process that can help you better understand the me you think you are.

(For more, see the next chapter: *In Pursuit of a Healthy Self-Esteem.*)

2. The me I wish I were
Do you wish you were someone else?

I wished that I was someone else for quite a long time. I wished, hoped, dreamed, and thought I was a rock star, Mr. Universe, or a movie star. I wished that I was rich and famous; I had all of the egotistical daydreams that you can think of. Dreaming and wishing to become something more than average is good, but only if it is followed by some action that will allow you to live out your dreams and wishes. Without taking some action to achieve them, our dreams give us nothing more than a false sense of hope and security.

2. The me I wish I were

Do you wish you were someone else?

One of the biggest problems that I encountered was that I spent too much time wishing and hoping, and not enough time actually doing. I realized today, while writing this, that I was not wishing to be anything other than the real me. Previously, I lacked the intuitive understanding that is vital to a healthy self-concept. I simply did not pay enough attention to the things that were important.

3. The me I really am
Who are you...really?

Each of us is many things all rolled up onto one. We are the unique experiences, influences, thoughts, commitments, goals, dreams, behaviors, and actions that allow us to be ourselves. Who is the real me? I am a man who practices every day the good things that I have learned. Even though I will make mistakes, I will do my best to avoid making ones that hurt the people I love. Who is the real you?

3. The me I really am

Who are you...really?

4. The me I try to project

Who and what are
you trying to project?

4. The me I try to project

Who and what are you trying to project?

Many of us try to project an image to others that is false. Those of you who knew me years ago know that I tried to project many different things, most of them lies. I disliked the real but 'average' me so much that I would make up stories of the things I had done in order to like myself more and to impress other people, to try and get them to like me. What happened, however, was quite different. They saw right through me, and I lost what little chance of having friends I may have had. A false sense of one's self creates another conflict to overcome in order to become more successful. I think that there are already enough things to overcome, don't you?

Don't you find that
people who project
a false sense of
themselves are easy
to see through?
What do you then
think about them?
Do you want to
befriend them?

A good example of this is people who try to project themselves as wealthy, when the truth is they don't have two dimes to rub together. Don't you find people who project a false sense of themselves easy to see through? What do you think about them then? Do you want to befriend them? Probably not.

You probably don't
want to be friends
with that person, right?
So if you are projecting
a false image of
yourself, don't you
think that other people
will see through you?
Do you think you are
that good at deceiving
yourself and others?

So, if you yourself are projecting a false image of yourself, don't you think that other people will see through you? Or do you think you are so good at deceiving other people and yourself that no one will notice? Don't fake it 'til you make it!

My advice? Project the me that you really are. Doing so means that you are being truthful to yourself and to others. Yes. Doing so takes a lot of integrity and courage, but the effects of being truthful to yourself and to others are greater than the consequences of lying to them and to yourself. When you do so, I bet you will find greater acceptance from others. In the end, you will have more friends and be more successful. You will enhance the quality of your life and the lives of the other people around you.

5. The me others perceive

How do other people perceive you? What do they think about when they mention your name?

Do you spend time worrying about how others will perceive you?

My advice? Project the real you and let other people perceive what they want to perceive. If the people that you want for friends don't like you for who you really are, find some new friends that do. Life is way too short to try and please everyone's perception of you by trying to fake it 'til you make it. This will only lead you to yet another conflict, resulting in a false sense of yourself and emptiness in your life.

6. The me I used to be

Who were you and have you changed at all in the last few years?

If you've learned anything useful from this book so far, you have undoubtedly changed. Some people can make drastic changes in their lives and make it seem simple, but some of us have a hard time changing even the smallest of things. Either way, no matter how hard it may seem, you can change. If you have changed at all, there is a "me that I used to be" in you.

Who were you? Are you at peace with the me that you used to be?

Some changes we can't control. Our physical bodies change as we get older. Our thoughts and perceptions change almost daily. Our values, wants, needs, and desires change. Our

5. The me others perceive

How do other people perceive you? What do they think about when they mention your name?

6. The me I used to be

Who were you? Have you changed at all in the last few years? If you have changed at all, is there a "me that I used to be" in you? What was it?

dreams and goals change. Our lifestyles change. I have learned that change is good and that most of the changes that we undergo are equally good. Personally, I have found that living *in* the past is unhealthy. Withing *with* the past is healthy. I now live with the fact that I am not who I used to be. Guess what? It's OK! That is the way it is. I have not forgotten who I was, but by dealing with it and being proud of who I was, I am able to have a healthier perspective of the me I used to be. Showing other people the "me I used to be" and the "me I am today" makes me proud of my past accomplishments and motivates me to become even better than I was before. Don't be afraid to let others know that you've changed. Learn to be proud of the me you used to be and other people will too.

I have found that living *in* the past is unhealthy. Living *with* the past is healthy.

7. The me others try to make me
What do other people want you to be?

7. The me others try to make me

What do other people want you to be?

For me, this was the toughest "me" to put into perspective. For years, I allowed other people to influence my life and career decisions. If you ask for advice for which you should already know the answer, you'll likely be answered by someone telling you about who they want you to be.

It's easy to sit back and let other people make the important decisions for us, to let them make us who they want us to be. If things don't work out as we would like, we have someone other than ourselves to blame for our failures and for not becoming and getting what we want out of our lives and our careers. Making intuitive and conscious decisions for ourselves regarding our happiness, who we want to be, and what we want to be is a basic requirement of successful living. It's our responsibility to our-

I have always wanted more out of my life and my career than what is good or average. I still do; do you?

selves to become who and what we want, no one else's. Author/speaker Tom Hopkins said it best when he said: "Being Happy is an individual responsibility. It's a duty you can not delegate."

Now, I am not telling you never to listen to the advice of others. I am merely suggesting that you combine their advice with what you know and intuitively feel to be truly what you want. Then make your own decisions about who and what you want to be, no matter what anyone else tells you! By making our own decisions, we take on the ultimate responsibility for our successes and failures in our lives.

Influences from the outside, like our family, boss, spouse, and environment, can be very powerful. Sometimes they are negatively powerful. If you are now or have been influenced by someone or something other than yourself to be or do something that you do not want, you will relate to this story well.

My father and everyone in my family are salespeople. He was (and still is) the best salesperson that I know. I think that he wanted me to follow in his footsteps and become a great salesperson as well. He influenced many of my decisions regarding my career path, which thankfully led me to become a successful salesman. I certainly headed down the wrong path more than once in my life, and he was there to help me when I needed him. I was afraid of making important decisions for myself regarding the me I wanted to be, so his influence was welcomed most of the time. Yes, he asked me many times who I really wanted to be and what I really wanted to do. However, I either did not have an answer that he liked, or even one that was 'feasible' at the time. I was always

Author/speaker Tom Hopkins said it best when he said: "Being Happy is an individual responsibility. It's a duty you can not delegate."

Do you make your life and career decisions for yourself, or are you under the influence of someone else?

looking too far into the future; I was dreaming about what and who I wanted to be instead of doing one thing at a time in pursuit of my dreams. He would often talk to me at great lengths to try and help me. He'd ask the right questions and I would answer with something like: "I don't know," or "I want to be a musician," or "I want to be in the movies." Invariably, I relayed some seemingly far-fetched idea, each one more unlike the "norm" than the one before. Here's the problem: It took me 29 years to tell him what I was going to do rather than ask what he thought I should do. No one but you can tell you what you want to do with your life.

I want more out of my life and my career than what is considered good or average. Do you?

All of the things that I wanted to do and be early on in my life were too far out for my family to handle. They were all more comfortable with what was considered the norm for a career path than a dream of being better than average. It still aggravates me to think that I allowed everyone to tell me what to do with my life and my career. I did not have the support that I needed to become more than "average" until I took it upon myself to make myself more than just average.

Do you make your life and career decisions for yourself? Or are you under the influence of someone else?

I've learned that each of us has a me they really want to be, and each of us has a me that others try to make us. When both of these are in perspective and in synch with each other, life is much more enjoyable and success is much more easily attained.

So, be who you want to be. Do what you want to do. Project the me you really are and let others see the real you. Don't forget the me you used to be, and do not allow others to try to make you be someone that you are not or influence your decisions about who and what you want to be. Find the courage and the strength to do and say what you really feel, and you will be successful. I believe that when we begin living a life and performing actions that do not conflict with our real me, we can anticipate and welcome both success and the pursuit thereof.

I found this "Happy Man's Creed" written in Napoleon Hill's book, *Success Through a Positive Mental Attitude*. I like it, and I hope you do too. I believe that it will inspire you to become closer to the real me inside of you.

Happy Man's Creed

The richest man in the world lives in Happy Valley. He is rich in values that endure, in things he cannot lose—things that provide him with contentment, sound health, peace of mind and harmony within his soul. Here is an inventory of his riches and how he acquired them: I found happiness by helping others to find it. I found sound health by living temperately and eating only the food my body requires to maintain itself. I hate no man, envy no man, but love and respect all mankind. I am engaged in a labor of love with which I mix play generously; therefore, I seldom grow tired. I pray daily, not for riches, but for more wisdom with which to recognize, embrace, and enjoy the great abundance of riches I already possess. I speak no name save only to honor it, and I slander no man for any cause whatsoever. I ask no favors of anyone except the privilege of sharing my blessings with all who desire them. I am on good terms with my conscience; therefore, it guides me accurately in everything I do. I have more material wealth than I need because I am free from greed and covet only those things I can use constructively while I live. My wealth comes from those whom I have benefited by sharing my blessings. The estate of Happy Valley which I own is not taxable. It exists mainly in my own mind, in intangible riches that cannot be assessed for taxation or appropriated except by those who adopt my way of life. I created this estate over a lifetime of effort by observing nature's laws and forming habits to conform to them.

(That's powerful, don't you think?)

Intuitive Consciousness and Our Energy!

Energy. All energy thrives on action. Everything is made of energy, some we can see and some we cannot. Some energy is intuited and exchanged through the encounters with people that occur every day. Sometimes, I find it difficult to harness and fully utilize my energy. Do you?

Some energy that we experience is intuited and exchanged through the encounters of our lives, and by the people that we meet every day.

Long hours spent working, and many nights spent worrying needlessly about business deals that were not life or death situations, drained me emotionally and physically of much of my energy. I think I've wasted much of my energy on things like worrying about what *might* happen instead of what I have to make happen. Do you?

I've found it is sometimes difficult to harness and fully utilize my energy. Have you?

Interestingly, as a result of practicing the thinking process that I call "Intuitive Consciousness," I slowly began to learn how to utilize my energies. Anyway, when I began to utilize my different energies, the quality of my work began to improve, along with the quality of my life. My days went more quickly, and my nights were spent snoozing away rather than tossing and turning.

Do you ever feel like you're just plain tired?

Imagine for a moment that you've worked all day and had a long miserable drive home in traffic. It rained all the way home, and traffic was a mess, to boot. The day before was the same, and the day before, and the day before that. As for sleep, you are not getting enough, and you often fall asleep at work. Exercise? What's exercise? That never crosses your mind because you're always tired. Can you identify with this scenario? Is it any wonder you are always tired and feel unsuccessful?

Do you ever feel like you're just plain tired?

THE FOUR ENERGIES

Let's explore the four energies that we all possess, Physical, Intellectual, Emotional, and Spiritual. Utilizing each of these energies will dramatically help you intuitively and consciously utilize their benefits, so you can refocus them on your success.

The Four Energies:

1. Physical

2. Intellectual

3. Emotional

4. Spiritual

Energy #1. Physical

Physical energy is the energy our bodies derive from nourishment by way of food. Our body simply is a machine that converts food energy into fuel for our muscles and our brain. Many of us suffer from a deficiency in physical energy, due mainly to a poor diet. When we eat junk, our actions are junk, and the things that we think about are junk. You know, if you put junk in your life you get junk out of your life.

Pretty simple right?

I recommend, at minimum, a moderate exercise program, which means 2–3 times per week for about 30 minutes. This will increase your ability to store, cycle, and convert physical energy, and it will make you look and feel great. It is amazing what happens when we do what comes naturally. Cycling physical energy through our bodies is a must do.

Energy #2. Intellectual

Intellectual energy. Our physical body must "cycle" energy through it to be an effective energy-converting machine. We must also cycle energy through our minds by way of intellectual stimulation. Simply reading a good book, having an in-depth conversation with a friend, or questioning a belief will do the job of cycling intellectual energy through your mind.

To stimulate my intellectual energy, I often engage in writing books or music, get into a good, heated discussion of a current topic of choice with a colleague, or go for a long walk and think, among many other things. Watching TV does not count!

When intellectual energy is cycled through our minds, it works them and expands our capability to think rationally. Try questioning some of your beliefs or solving a huge problem. The idea is to make yourself use your intellectual energy.

Energy #3. Emotional

Emotional energy can be both positive and negative. Whether the energy is positive or negative depends upon your mood and attitude at the time. It is very much an individual perception. Using the process that I have described as "Intuitive Consciousness," we can learn how better to control our positive and negative emotional energy expenditures. We can then better understand how anger, fear, anxiety, depression, remorse, and the events of our daily lives can produce feelings and emotions that affect us in different ways.

Emotional energy can be described in three ways: first, as an attitude; second, as a feeling or intuition; and third, as an emotion. Each of these is contagious. When a group of people laughs, for example, the laughter—and the emotion that accompanies it—is contagious. This can be seen when we laugh at television sitcoms we think are funny. When the laughter starts in the background audience on the TV show, we naturally pick up on the positive energy and also laugh.

According to a book written by James Redfield, entitled *The Celestine Prophecy*, a person's energy, or "energy field," can actually be seen. I know it can be felt, but I have yet to see anyone's "energy field." Although I have not seen one, I do not doubt that this is true.

I've often met people who gave me a certain emotional *feeling* or intuition the moment that I either saw or met them. Have you?

That feeling is the feeling of energy. That being the case, it only made sense when, as I read further, Redfield's book described a process of energy being projected onto other things and other people. This explains my earlier statement that energy or attitudes are contagious and are felt when people meet.

It is critically important to develop an intuitive awareness that our emotions can cause us to deplete or store our energy. We must then make a conscious effort to harness them. For example, when emotions like fear and anger are felt, we produce negative energy, which quickly depletes our energy. Have you ever noticed how much energy you expend when you are angry? Does being angry, even for a short period of time, make you really tired?

Just a few short minutes of anger can leave us completely drained of our energy. However,

> I've often met people who gave me a certain *feeling* the moment that I either saw or met them. Have you?

Have you ever noticed how much energy you expend when you are angry? Does being angry, even for a short period of time, make you really tired?

when emotions and feelings like love, happiness, fulfillment, and joy are felt they seem to produce an almost endless supply of energy for us to draw upon.

My point here is simply this: If you deter negative emotions, you will deter negative energy consumption, and you will deter the depletion of the energy that you need in order to become successful.

Energy #4. Spiritual

Spiritual energy. I am no expert on spiritual energy. I have only recently begun to study, experiment, and understand the concepts of spiritual energy. If you define spiritual energy as Godly, you will find few direct references in this book to it in that form. I now believe in a higher being, and I am learning more about spiritual energy every day. What I do know to be true is that a simple belief in Jesus Christ and in God seems to have had a mysterious and positive effect on me and my life; one I can only quantify as the Holy Spirit. Can anyone really define it? Amazingly, the belief itself brings about an increase in the vitality and the quality of my entire life. I now attribute much of my success to prayers that have been answered.

If you define spiritual energy as that thing within all of us that makes us who we are and drives us to be successful, then you will find many references to spiritual energy in this book. Maybe you already know about spiritual energy. How has it positively affected your life and career?

Perhaps when I understand spiritual energy from a more enlightened point of view, I will share my thoughts with you in another book.

Until that day, I will shut up and learn. I suggest you consult an authority on the subject to find out more. That is exactly what I am going to do.

Cycling Our Energy

A main reason many of us suffer from a deficiency of energy is that we do not regularly use, or "cycle," our physical energy. Too many of us sit behind our computers all day long instead of doing what comes naturally: cycling energy through our minds, spirits, and bodies. Cycling energy is the natural process for our minds, spirits, and bodies to perform. They simply convert food energy—the food we eat—to physical energy, the things that we do. The human mind and body are made to take in energy, cycle it through, store the leftovers, and expel the waste.

Now, since many of us are not cycling energy through our minds and bodies, we simply lose the ability to convert, store, and cycle energy. It's sort of the "use it or lose it" theory. This can be substantiated by examining how the body's metabolism slows down when we do not exercise regularly. As we get older, the process becomes more difficult to control, because everything seems to slow down.

USING THE 50%–75%–150% RULE
FOR BEING "ON"

Assume for a moment, if you will, that you have just gotten out of bed to begin your day. It's nothing special, just another ordinary day. For whatever reason, you just cannot seem to get it together like you normally do. The kids are late; there is no time for breakfast; the dog is peeing on the carpet because you forgot to let him out;

the buttons on your shirt popped off—you get the point—everything seems to be going wrong. You can tell that it's going to be "one of those days."

You normally have an unbridled, 150%, "go for it" attitude and an endless energy supply; for whatever reason, you just do not feel fired up today. We all have those days when everything we do seems to go wrong and we cannot seem to get going in a positive direction. These are the days when we are at about 50% of our maximum capacity for work and daily life. This is natural, it happens to all of us from time to time.

What is not natural is how we beat ourselves up over it, which makes things even worse.

Then there are those days when we are "on"; we're at 150% of our maximum capacity, making our best decisions and doing our best work. You know what I mean, those days when you seem to do no wrong; you can feel it, and everyone can see it on your face; those days when we seem to have an endless supply of energy to draw from, energy that allows you to tackle the really tough projects and make the really hard decisions with ease.

One of the biggest mistakes that can be made is not to realize when you are "on" and when you are "off." We push ourselves to be "on" when we are not mentally and physically capable of being "on." This causes a great deal of problems, such as anxiety, depression, and unhappiness.

What I have learned to do through intuitively listening to myself and consciously making good decisions is to know when, and when not, to push myself to do my best. I have learned to quickly determine what my intuitions are, and how I feel at any given time. Then I make a conscious decision to match my work level for that particular time and day based upon how I feel. I determine whether I am "on," at 50%, 75%, or 150%.

When I do not feel "on," or I feel like I am at only 50% or 75% of my maximum capacity, I do not try to do more than I can. When I feel pure, unbridled energy, when I am at 150% of my maximum capacity and everything is working great, I push myself as hard as I can. I want to do my best work then, not when I am in an "off," or 50%, mode. When we are really "on" is the time to make all of the tough decisions, problem-solve, and tackle all of the really big projects that we have to do. I simply save the really important things and decisions for the days when I am really "on," really hitting on all cylinders, and when I feel like I am at 150% of my maximum capacity.

Does it not make sense, then, to intuit your ability to do your best by the day, and then make conscious decisions to set up your life, work, and fun around how you feel at any given time?

At first glace you may think that this is silly, but allow me to explain further. Can you honestly say that you are at 150% of your maximum capacity to do your best all of the time, every day? At one consistent level all the time? Of course not. No one can be. We all have days when we are "on" 150%, and days when we are "off" 50%. So does it not then make sense to intuit your ability to do your best by the day and make a conscious decision to set up your life, work, and fun around how feel at any given time? Sure it does. If you average 50%, 75%, and 150% you get 95% right? Well, if all we did was function at an average rate of 95% of our maximum capacity, we would actually end up doing more quality work and having more fun in life than if we tried to push ourselves when we were not "on."

When I began to use the 50%–75%–150% rule, I began to have fewer and fewer days where I was only at 50% or 75% of my max, because I did not push myself when I was not capable of doing my best. Pushing too hard when we are not ready makes things worse and raises our level of stress. I've experienced less and less anxiety, unhappiness, and depression, and that alone has increased my ability to do better work for longer periods of time before I get stressed out.

If you put junk in your mind, you get junk out of your life.

Actually, when we push ourselves to do our best and are not really "on," we set ourselves up for frustrating disappointments which lead to depression, stress, and anxiety. Ultimately, it leads to a substantial decrease in our ability to perform well. We can't possibly do our best when we are not "on"; and when we realize that we are not doing our best, we beat ourselves up over it. What happens next is typical. Frustration leads to anger, which then leads to anxiety, which then leads to depression, which ultimately leads to burnout.

Take today, for example. I can feel that I am at about 75% of my maximum capacity to do my best. I am only capable of short spurts of intense work, usually about an hour at a time, then I need a short break. So, I do not plan to make any real tough decisions today, unless things change. All I want to do today is get through this chapter, sort through some easy decisions, make a few phone calls, and relax at the end of the evening. I have consciously made the decisions to save the real tough stuff for either later this afternoon when I feel "on," or for tomorrow, when I may feel 150% of my maximum capacity to do my best. This little breather allows me to gain control and focus on pulling the day out of the junk pile without putting a tremendous amount of pressure on myself.

Another reason many of us suffer from a deficiency of physical energy is that we do not regularly use or "cycle" our physical energy by way of exercise.

Each of us has an optimum pattern or energy cycle for each and every day. It has been referred to by some as "biorhythms"; you can call it what you want. The fact is, some of us are morning people, who tend to do our best work in the morning. Some of us are night people and do our best work at night. Others do their best in the afternoon. If you are like me, you have short spurts of unbridled energy throughout the day or night, sometimes all day, sometimes all night, sometimes not at all. For example, I tend to do some of my best work at night or on days around 8AM–10AM, 1PM–4PM, and 7PM–12PM. In between these times, I need some controlled laziness—some time to do the little things throughout the day that cause me no grief and that are easy.

One of the biggest mistakes that we make is that, for a variety of reasons, we do not realize when we are "on" or "off," yet we push ourselves to be and do more than we are capable of at a given time.

So if you are a morning person and you do your best work in the morning, save all of the really tough stuff that you have to do for the morning. Don't try to do your really tough things in the afternoon when you are not at your best. Don't waste your morning with trivial stuff like opening the mail! Makes sense, huh? If you are like me and you generally get several short spurts of unbridled energy and controlled focus through-out the day, then pace yourself and do one major thing at a time. Use your breaks away from the tough stuff to do the easy stuff.

HOW TO DETERMINE YOUR OPTIMUM ENERGY PATTERN

Each day for a period of ten days, write down the exact times of each day that you experience either 50%, 75%, or 150% energy cycling or feelings that you can do your best. Make sure that you note exactly how long each one of the cycles lasts, even if it is only ten minutes long. Also, note anything that happens to affect each energy cycle, such as arguments, big projects, and especially those things that you can directly attribute to causing the energy cycle to go up or down.

At the end of the ten days, review your notes and findings. You should be able to identify a pattern for each "on" 150% and "off" 75% and 50% energy cycle for each day. What you will be looking for are similarities in energy cycles throughout each day or for a majority of days in the week. When you have identified a pattern for your "on" and "off" energy cycles, you will have identified your optimum energy cycling pattern. For example, if you notice that around 9:00AM each day you feel "on" (150%), schedule your tough assignments and the things that you really need to concentrate on for 9:00AM each day. If you find through your research that you feel "off" (50%) around 2:00PM each day, don't schedule your important tasks around 2:00PM unless you must. If you find that you are like me, and generally have several one-hour spurts of focused energy throughout the day, set up your daily routine so that you can complete several important projects throughout the day; then fill in your "off" or 50%–75% times with the easy stuff that you have to do.

Finally, begin setting up your daily schedule around your peak "on" and "off" energy cycles for each day. This strategy will dramatically improve the quality of your life and your work.

Use this form to determine your optimum energy pattern.

Identify all periods of "ON" 150%, 75%, and "OFF" 50% energy cycles throughout each of the following days. You're looking for a definite pattern—some similarities.

Day 1

AM   NOTES

    7–7:30 _____

    8–8:30 _____

    9–9:30 _____

  10–10:30 _____

  11–11:30 _____

PM

12–12:30 _____

    1–1:30 _____

    2–2:30 _____

    3–3:30 _____

    4–4:30 _____

    5–5:30 _____

    6–6:30 _____

    7–7:30 _____

    8–8:30 _____

    9–9:30 _____

  10–10:30 _____

Day 2

AM   NOTES

    7–7:30 _____

    8–8:30 _____

    9–9:30 _____

  10–10:30 _____

  11–11:30 _____

PM   NOTES

12–12:30   _____

1–1:30   _____

2–2:30   _____

3–3:30   _____

4–4:30   _____

5–5:30   _____

6–6:30   _____

7–7:30   _____

8–8:30   _____

9–9:30   _____

10–10:30   _____

Day 3

AM   NOTES

7–7:30   _____

8–8:30   _____

9–9:30   _____

10–10:30   _____

11–11:30   _____

PM

12–12:30   _____

1–1:30   _____

2–2:30   _____

3–3:30   _____

4–4:30   _____

5–5:30   _____

PM   NOTES

6–6:30   _____

7–7:30   _____

8–8:30   _____

9–9:30   _____

10–10:30 _____

Day 4

AM   NOTES

7–7:30   _____

8–8:30   _____

9–9:30   _____

10–10:30 _____

11–11:30 _____

PM

12–12:30 _____

1–1:30   _____

2–2:30   _____

3–3:30   _____

4–4:30   _____

5–5:30   _____

6–6:30   _____

7–7:30   _____

8–8:30   _____

9–9:30   _____

10–10:30 _____

Day 5

AM   NOTES

7–7:30   _____

8–8:30   _____

9–9:30   _____

10–10:30 _____

11–11:30 _____

PM

12–12:30 _____

1–1:30   _____

2–2:30   _____

3–3:30   _____

4–4:30   _____

5–5:30   _____

6–6:30   _____

7–7:30   _____

8–8:30   _____

9–9:30   _____

10–10:30 _____

Day 6

AM   NOTES

7–7:30   _____

8–8:30   _____

9–9:30   _____

10–10:30 _____

11–11:30 _____

PM   NOTES

12–12:30 _____

1–1:30   _____

2–2:30   _____

3–3:30   _____

4–4:30   _____

5–5:30   _____

6–6:30   _____

7–7:30   _____

8–8:30   _____

9–9:30   _____

10–10:30 _____

Day 7

AM   NOTES

7–7:30   _____

8–8:30   _____

9–9:30   _____

10–10:30 _____

11–11:30 _____

PM

12–12:30 _____

1–1:30   _____

2–2:30   _____

3–3:30   _____

4–4:30   _____

5–5:30   _____

PM   NOTES

6–6:30   _____

7–7:30   _____

8–8:30   _____

9–9:30   _____

10–10:30 _____

Day 8

AM   NOTES

7–7:30   _____

8–8:30   _____

9–9:30   _____

10–10:30 _____

11–11:30 _____

PM

12–12:30 _____

1–1:30   _____

2–2:30   _____

3–3:30   _____

4–4:30   _____

5–5:30   _____

6–6:30   _____

7–7:30   _____

8–8:30   _____

9–9:30   _____

10–10:30 _____

Day 9

AM   NOTES

7–7:30   _____

8–8:30   _____

9–9:30   _____

10–10:30 _____

11–11:30 _____

PM

12–12:30 _____

1–1:30   _____

2–2:30   _____

3–3:30   _____

4–4:30   _____

5–5:30   _____

6–6:30   _____

7–7:30   _____

8–8:30   _____

9–9:30   _____

10–10:30 _____

Day 10

AM   NOTES

7–7:30   _____

8–8:30   _____

9–9:30   _____

10–10:30 _____

11–11:30 _____

PM	NOTES
12–12:30	_____
1–1:30	_____
2–2:30	_____
3–3:30	_____
4–4:30	_____
5–5:30	_____
6–6:30	_____
7–7:30	_____
8–8:30	_____
9–9:30	_____
10–10:30	_____

BALANCING THE FIVE ASPECTS OF INTUITIVE CONSCIOUSNESS

Identifying the five aspects—work, fun, relationships, self, and our energies—was the easy part. Balancing, mastering, practicing, and living by them was hard. Here's how I made it easier:

First, I wrote down each of the five aspects on a separate piece of paper. At the beginning of each day, I put all five pieces in my left pants pocket. Then, throughout the day, I made it a point to do something regarding each of the five aspects. Each time that I did that, I moved the piece of paper from my left pocket to my right pocket.

At the end of the day, I would see how many of the pieces of paper wound up in my right pants pocket. In a matter of 2–3 weeks, I began to train myself to do something for each of the five aspects every day. What a difference in my life this has made! Try it for yourself.

CHAPTER 9

IN PURSUIT OF A HEALTHY
SELF-ESTEEM

How do you feel about yourself? What do you think of when you think of you?

I've had more than my share of days when I thought that I was worthless and that I wanted to quit and die. What I have learned to do through experience is to practice thinking of myself in a positive way. I also learned how important it is to do this regularly. Let this section serve as a starting point, a reference point that will help you begin a process of building a healthier, realistic, and confident self-esteem.

How do you feel about yourself? What do you think of when you think of you?

To build a healthier self-esteem, you have to be living and performing positively. If you are doing things that are wrong to others and to yourself, you will find it very hard to think positively about yourself and have a healthy self-esteem. However, if you are living and performing successful habits for your life and your career, and you are acting in other people's good interest, it will be much easier to feel, think, and act positively about yourself.

We tend to put on a good show, portraying what we lead ourselves to believe are successful thoughts and actions, when all the while we secretly have a very low self-esteem and think that we are worthless.

For years, I lived with a false sense of self-esteem and self-worth. Many of us tend to put on a good show, portraying what we lead ourselves to believe are successful thoughts about ourselves, when all the while we secretly have a very low self-esteem, and think we are worthless. It's yet another of the conflicts that we face in pursuit of success. It's easier to pretend to be confident than to stop things long enough to look inside ourselves to see and feel what and who is the real truth.

What and who is your real truth? I believe before we can achieve true success, we must overcome this conflict that exists within ourselves. When we have properly dealt with our feelings regarding ourselves, success will be achieved. It is a process I have found to be very painful and enjoyable at the same time.

When I truly began to see myself as successful (not anything grandiose) through performing positive thoughts and actions in my life and my career, I began to have a healthier self-esteem. It changed my life. Dealing rationally with your feelings of self-worth will result in successful habits, increased self-confidence, and powerful thoughts and actions. You will exude success. Yes, I still have to practice feeling good about myself every day.

Try to think of yourself as being *good* at what you do—not the *best* at what you do. Why is this a healthy perspective? Because there is always someone better than you are. Be happy with what you have gotten accomplished to date, and stop trying to keep up with the Joneses. Realistic and confident self-esteem is achieved by losing your narcissistic attitude! Live up to your own potential, not your neighbor's.

"Sow an action and you reap a habit; sow a habit and you reap a character; sow a character and you reap a destiny."

—William James

> If you are living and performing successful habits for your life and your career, and you are acting in other people's good interest, it will be much easier to feel, think, and act positively about yourself.

> It is critically important to practice thinking of yourself as *good* at what you do—not the *best* at what you do. Why is this a healthy perspective?

Eight Ways to Build a Healthier Self-esteem

Each strategy for building a healthier self-esteem requires you to do something. What are you going to do?

1. *Stop comparing yourself to anyone but you!*

Success and happiness are not measured by how well you do compared to anyone but you. In other words, are you living up to your own potential to succeed? Not the potential of the people who you work with or the potential they expect from you, but rather the potential that you expect from yourself? You can do better than you are doing right now if you choose to, can't you? I believe that you can!

Hey! Take a break and be easy on yourself for a change. You can't do everything as well as everyone else, but there are some things that you do well and better than others. Remember this... You don't have to *be* the best to be successful, you simply have to *try* to be your best to be successful.

2. *Learn how to take a compliment with sincerity!*

Compliments from others are meant to tell you how well you are doing, not how bad at everything you are. When you do not take a compliment from others well, they will stop giving them to you. If you said to a friend or colleague: "Good job," and they responded with "no big deal," or "I was just lucky, I wish I could do that all the time," how would this comment make you feel? Less likely to compliment that person again, right? If someone you complimented insulted you, would you continue to compliment them?

Each strategy for building a healthier self-esteem requires you to do something. What are you going to do?

Remember this... You don't have to *be* the best to be successful, you simply have to *try* to be your best in order to be successful.

Eight strategies for effective self-esteem building:

1. Stop comparing yourself to anyone but yourself!

2. Learn how to take a compliment with sincerity!

By not taking a compliment graciously with a simple statement like "Thank you," or "Thanks, I will try to do it again," or "Thanks, here is how I did it," you put yourself down and insult the person that is complimenting you. Don't be afraid to take some credit when credit is due. The next time someone gives you a compliment, try saying: "Thank you," and keep on trying your best.

3. Become a 'giver' not a 'taker'!

This is a successity! It's an absolute success necessity!

How can we feel good about ourselves and have a healthy self-esteem when we don't help other people? After all, helping other people is the essence of successful living.

I don't think that we can. By not volunteering some of your time to help other people and by not giving people simple compliments through-out each day, whether you receive one or not, you violate every success law imaginable. I believe that being a giver and not a taker is one of the most powerful things that we can do to build a healthy self-esteem. (See the section "The power of giving to others and leaving the narcissism behind" for more.) By the way, I said volunteering, no payment for helping others allowed!

4. Stop kicking yourself when you're down!

All of us, at one time or another, have put ourselves down. What is really detrimental to our self-esteem is making a habit of it. As our self-esteem begins to drop, we have a tendency to stomp on it, which makes everything seem worse than it really is. The logical thing to do is to be more intuitively and consciously aware of the fact that you are more susceptible to negative thinking and feelings of a low self-esteem when you are down. At that critical time, pay more attention to how you feel about yourself, and avoid beating yourself up over the little things.

When we say things about ourselves that are negative, like "I'm no good at anything," or "I can't do anything right," it only reinforces our feelings of low self-esteem. So, instead of wasting your energy thinking about the things that are going bad and kicking yourself for them, try thinking of the good things that you have going on. If you stop putting yourself down long enough to see the real you and see past the superficial issues at hand, you will find a great person inside you just waiting to get out. Look for the good in you! We all have the ability to "do it right," and to "do it good." We are each born with the capability of doing well. Do not waste your time or energy thinking about the bad stuff. Most of the bad stuff that we think about is b.s. and does not really matter anyway! If it's not life or death, it's not worth worrying about!

5. *Confirm the good qualities that you already have!*

5. Confirm the good qualities that you already have!

It is really easy to sit there and say to yourself "I'm no good," or "I can't do anything right," isn't it?

Just as you will read about planning your life and career out with a written plan of action later in this book, you must periodically do an inventory of your good and bad qualities. This confirms your good qualities and feelings by simply planning them out and writing them down.

Try writing down everything that you do well on one side of a piece of paper, and everything that you do not do well on the other side. Remember, don't compare yourself to anyone but you. Your list should be *your* list—influenced by no one but you. Do not get someone to help you with it; do it yourself. On your list, include your good qualities, feelings, and accomplishments. Your list will help you confirm the good qualities that you really have and will serve as a way to inventory and confirm them.

After you complete your list, focus your energy on the things that you are best at and put them to work for you right now! Don't waste any more time!

As for the bad qualities that you identify on your list, simply make them the part of your list that you need to improve on. Try reviewing your "bad qualities to work on" list 2–3 times per day for a week or so. Put a little extra effort into improving the bad qualities that you have identified. Within a week or so you will see that you are not as crummy as you thought you were, and that you can change that bad stuff that you identified into good stuff.

6. Use the power of
your mind in a
positive way with
positive affirmations!

6. *Use the power of your mind in a positive way with positive affirmations!*

Positive affirmations like: "I'm doing better," or "I can do this," or "yes I can," can be a powerful way to build a healthy self-esteem when they are said with emotion. Just saying the words is not enough. They have to be said with emotion and conviction, out loud!

Try writing down two or three positive affirmations of your choice and taping them to the dash of your car. Every time you get in the car, read each affirmation. Then say each one with emotion! Yell it out as loud as you can! After you try it a few times it will not seem as silly as it sounds, it really works.

7. *Allocate some time to do what you are good at and enjoy doing!*

7. Allocate some time to do what you are good at and enjoy doing!

Becoming successful can be a living hell or it can be a magnificent adventure. I know. I've been through both. The choice is yours. Personally, I like a good adventure.

Which would you like?

What do you do well? What do you enjoy doing other than work? Whatever it is, do it often in order to build yourself a healthy self-esteem.

Don't spend a large portion of your life, as I did, doing things that you constantly have to work at to be good, like work. Allocate some time to do the things that you are good at or that you enjoy doing. If you think you are not good at anything or don't enjoy anything, **find something that you like to do, quickly!** This strategy will help you reconfirm to yourself that you can do some things well. It will help you balance the things you are good at and the things that you need to work on to get better.

8. Be a person of action!

8. *Be a person of action!*

Whatever you do, do not sit around waiting for something or someone to make you feel better!

Do you measure yourself and your success by your actions?

Do you measure yourself and your success by your actions?

You should. Because it is your actions—the things that you do and the things that you do not do—that determine the level of success that you achieve and the positive feelings you can feel about yourself.

How can we feel good about ourselves and have a healthy self-esteem when we don't help other people? After all, helping other people is the essence of successful living, right?

It is real easy to say to yourself: "I'm no good," or "I can't do anything right," when you don't feel good about yourself, isn't it?

What do you like to do? What do you do well? What do you enjoy doing other than work?

The worst thing that you can do for a low self-esteem is sit around and do nothing.

The worst thing that you can do for a low self-esteem is sit around and do nothing. You make it easy to have feelings of a low self-esteem when you do nothing. You see, it is what we do, it's our actions in our lives and at home, in our work and in our relationships, that determine how we feel about ourselves and how successful we become. Let's assume that you are a salesperson. The worst thing that you can do after being rejected ten times is to go home and sulk. You are better off making sales calls until you make a sale. It's amazing how getting one sale can turn a whole week around.

I had trouble being a person of action until I made the simple decision to try and do new things. If you are having problems being a 'doer' or a person of action, I know what it feels like. I had trouble doing even the most mundane tasks that we all must do to live and exist, and I sometimes still do. Actually, I am a play, baby; I like to have fun.

This strategy is probably the most important strategy of all: you must do something, take some action towards changing the way that things are. What will you do?

This strategy is probably the most important strategy of all. Why? Because each of the previous ones requires you to do something, to take some action. You must do something, take some action toward changing the way that things are. What will you do?

What's next?

Do something. Anything! Try something new and exciting! Break out of that comfort zone and that same old routine. Stop being afraid to try something new. Stop it! It's that easy! There are some really neat people to meet and some awesome things to see on this planet. Some will make you very happy and will accept you for the way that you really are. So go out and find them! I will make you this one promise—you will not find them sitting on your butt on your couch watching television and eating potato chips!

If you feel that performing and utilizing one of the previous eight strategies is too much for you to do and you need a "quick fix" to build up your self-esteem, try one of the following strategies. Any one of these will help provide you with a sense of enthusiasm for successful living and boost your self-esteem.

Self-esteem "Quick Fixes"

1. Get a haircut.

Do you get enhanced feelings of positive self-esteem after a haircut? I do. I seem to view myself a little better looking—you know, a little more appetizing—after a haircut. Caution. Make sure before you leave the salon that you are happy with the haircut!

2. Have sex! Enough said?

3. Tell someone that you love them!

What a good feeling it is to know that you have told someone that you love them. This should be a part of your everyday schedule!

4. Read or listen to motivational material.

When I begin feeling the effects of a low self-esteem, I have to turn off any and all negative influences, and I either read or listen to my motivational material. After all, I created it for the person who needed it the most at the time of creation: me. Sometimes I write some new material; it depends upon my particular mood at the time and what my needs may be. I know beyond a shadow of a doubt that this strategy is effective at making your feelings of low self-esteem go away. Reading and listening to motivational material should also be a part of your everyday

Simply put, if you put junk in, you'll get junk out. If you put good stuff like motivational material in your mind, you'll get good, positive stuff out!

schedule. I tend to think of this kind of material as "vitamins for the mind, soul, and spirit." Simply put, if you put junk in, you'll get junk out. If you put good stuff in your mind, like motivational material, you'll get good stuff out!

5. Try some exercise!

I'm not talking about going to the gym and sweating your butt off; I'm just talking about some general exercise like walking, riding a bike, swimming, or working in the yard. Personally, I can't live without some exercise every other day. Although I am not the physical specimen that I once was, I can reconfirm my commitment to myself to stay in some form of good physical shape by exercising a minimum of every other day. It boosts my self-esteem by making me look and feel great. Feeling great is the way that we build a high tolerance for the negative things that happen to us in life. It helps provide us with a generous amount of internal courage, hope, and optimism. All for a better self-esteem.

CHAPTER 10

THREE STRATEGIES

PROGRAMMING AND REPROGRAMMING THE MIND FOR SUCCESS

TAKE BACK CONTROL OF YOUR MIND!

Review & Quotes & for Your Notes

Take back control of your mind! I like to think of this section of the book as boot camp for the mind. Programming and reprogramming your conscious and subconscious minds is where your untapped powers to perform successfully are hidden. Make a commitment to learn how to utilize them both. This section will help you learn how to do it.

Programming and reprogramming your conscious and subconscious minds is where your untapped powers to perform successfully are hidden.

Becoming successful is a state of mind that becomes a way of life. It is attained through the completion of successful habits for your life and your career. You see, it's what and how we think that actually makes us successful. Probably the greatest obstacle that you will have to overcome in order to become more successful will be your present mindset. You must learn how to change the way that you think and what you think.

Success is mostly a state of mind that becomes a way of life and is pursued through the completion of successful habits for your life and your career.

I have identified three strategies that I believe will help you program and reprogram your mind for success. As with all strategies that lead

Three Strategies
for programming and
reprogramming
the mind:

1. Change what you
associate with pain
and pleasure.

2. Use positive
affirmations.

3. Deter negative
influences.

According to many
psychologists,
many of the things that
we do are in response to
the two most powerful
sensations that we
can experience,
pain and pleasure.

We must learn not to
focus on how painful
taking action will be.
Instead, we must learn
to focus on how
painful *not taking*
action will be.

to success, you will have to take some action and practice them, then master them for best results.

Strategy 1: Change what you associate with pain and pleasure.

According to many psychologists, many of the things that we do are in response to the two most powerful sensations that we can experience, pain and pleasure. This is commonly referred to in psycho-babble terminology as the "Pain and Pleasure Principle." These two powerful sensations can control us. They can dominate our actions. Our response to either of these controls what we feel, how we act, how we perform, and what we think.

As we think and learn, we begin to associate these two sensations with our beliefs. We then make our decisions based upon whether our actions will bring us pain or pleasure. I believe that it is our mistaken responses to pain and pleasure that are the most notable of the underlying reasons we have difficulty in making successful changes, decisions, and adding or taking away habits in our lives and in our careers.

You see, we have become "conditioned" to associate successful habits with pain rather than with pleasure. Consequently, we don't associate many of our daily work activities and habits with pleasure. How do we fix the problem? We must learn not to focus on how painful *taking* action will be. Instead, we must learn to focus on how painful *not taking* action will be.

Here is an example of the pain and pleasure principle: If you are in sales, and you want to make more sales today and every day hereafter, you must focus on how painful NOT making your best sales calls every day will be rather than wasting your energy focusing on how painful making sales calls will be. Ask yourself what's more painful: making sales calls and making more money? Or not making sales calls, making nothing, and losing your job? Common sense would tell you that not making sales calls and losing your job would be more painful. When you begin to associate less pain and more pleasure with making sales calls, you will be dramatically more successful and happier with your career as a salesperson.

Have you ever used the excuse, "I don't want to drive all the way over to that account; the buyer is never in"? Heck, I know that I've made more than my share of excuses not to work. In order to change the way that things are and make them better, you must begin to link or reassociate pleasure with successful work habits, like sales calls, travel, cold calls, telephoning, and new account prospecting. If you are a true salesperson and not an order taker, it should be pleasurable for you to make sales calls, knowing that you will be making the big bucks and seeing clients who are your close friends.

I, too, have made the mistake of associating pain with making sales calls, especially in some of my early career opportunities, which required me to make 15–20 cold calls per day! To fix the problem, I simply reassociated making sales calls with pleasure rather than pain. After thinking about it intuitively and consciously, I realized that it would be more painful not to make sales calls. You see, I simply had to evaluate which was MORE painful. Making sales calls and becoming successful? Or not making sales calls and losing everything that I had? Obviously the thought

> Remember, you can have more than you've got—because you can become more than you are.

> If you are in sales and you want to make more sales today and every day, you must focus on how painful NOT making your best sales calls every day will be.

of losing everything that I had was more painful for me, and I began to make more and better sales calls. All I really did was change my perception of sales calls. No longer did sales calls seem painful, nor did the rest of the job requirements. This one simple strategy has helped me tremendously.

Reassociating pain and pleasure works for any kind of change you want to make regarding how and what you think. You can add or delete any habit in your life or your career. You can stop smoking, lose weight, or change whatever you want, once you change your thinking. When we begin changing what we associate with pain and pleasure, we stop allowing our environment, surroundings, and our conditioned responses to make our life and career decisions for us. We stop winging it. So, begin right NOW! Begin associating pleasure with successful work habits. Remember, you can have more than you've got, because you can become more than you are.

Strategy 2: Using positive affirmations

It's what and how we think and believe, both consciously and subconsciously, and what we associate our thoughts and actions with, that ultimately drive us to be successful.

> We translate into physical reality the thoughts and attitudes which we hold in our minds, no matter what they are. But when our attitude towards ourselves is big, and our attitude towards others is generous and merciful, we attract big and generous portions of success.
>
> —Napoleon Hill,
> *Success Through a Positive Mental Attitude*

So, what's a positive affirmation? It's nothing more than a simple statement, one you either make up or read elsewhere, that helps to spark your own self-motivation.

Consciously performed positive affirmations, used with intensity and emotion, solidify into subconscious auto-suggestions that motivate you to take action. They flash from your subconscious mind to your conscious mind to help motivate you at your time of need.

For example, when I exercise and it begins to tax my body's mental and physical capabilities, I often have to use a positive affirmation to continue when I feel like stopping. I often tell myself: "Come on Joe, you can do anything for ten more minutes." Undoubtedly there are times when I would have never made it through some of my workouts without an affirmation from myself that I could do what I was doing for just a little while longer.

Here's another example. Early in my selling career I was working for a company that required everyone to make at least 15 cold calls per day, rain or shine. So, when making those cold calls, I would often have to use positive affirmations to keep me going when I really wanted to just quit and go home. This simple and motivating positive affirmation helped me keep on making calls when I wanted to quit, and it made me a star: "Come on man, you can do better than this, so focus—focus! You can do this, you can sell this prospect—don't quit now; you're not a quitter!"

Use this space to create your own positive affirmation and use it whenever you need it to get you through the tough times while you pursue success, those times when you think you cannot continue, and you want to quit.

Strategy 3: Deter negative influences

Have you ever noticed how being around someone who is negative makes you negative too?

This is because attitudes are contagious. People who are miserable make everyone around them miserable too. Their cynicism and pessimistic

Have you ever noticed how being around someone who is negative makes you negative too?

attitudes are simply a bad influence on you, and what a powerfully bad influence they can be! Positive influences can positively change your attitude and lead you to be positive. People are not the only bad influence on you. Other things that are negative influences include some television programs, like the news, and some of the things that you may read.

Here's how to begin deterring negative influences.

To deter negative influences, first surround yourself with other people that have positive attitudes. Then follow by weeding out all the negative stuff, both in your life at home and your life at work.

First, surround yourself with people that have positive attitudes. Don't hang around losers with loser attitudes! Follow up by weeding out all the negative stuff, both in your life at home and your life at work. Being around other people who consistently have positive thoughts and who are happy will rub off on you, making you happy. I simply do not spend time around people who are unhappy or who have negative, whiney attitudes. This strategy involves taking a close look at who you call your friends.

Now that you have weeded out the people that are negative, move on to weeding out the rest of your negative influences. Here are some good places to start: work, television, the Internet, video games, and some movies.

You will be amazed at what a difference in your life and your career this one simple strategy will make. Simply put, if you are among negative influences long enough, eventually your attitude can become negative too. In other words, if you put junk in your mind, you'll get junk out of your mind! Enough said?

CHAPTER 11

CLEANSING OUR CONSCIOUSNESS

EMPTYING OUR MENTAL TRASH CANS

Is your consciousness clear? Is your mental trash can so full that it does not allow you to continue searching for life's basic pleasures? What is a mental trash can?

It's our conscious and subconscious minds. Cleansing our consciousness and emptying our mental trash cans are significantly important. If you ever have feelings of remorse about some of the bad things that you have done (which you should), you may be experiencing an unnecessary amount of guilt and anxiety. These feelings can make our lives utterly miserable, and the lives of those around us miserable, too. For me, the process of cleansing my consciousness and emptying my mental trash can was very humiliating and painful. Yet, for all the shame and pain that I suffered, I reaped rewards a thousand times over.

Anxiety and remorse created by an unclear conscience can literally kill a career. Before I could start my consulting company, I felt like I had to leave the past behind me for good. I felt like I had to make restitution for the many things that I'd done wrong both to myself and to others

Review & Quotes & for Your Notes

Is your consciousness clear? Is your mental trash can full, not allowing you to continue a search for life's basic pleasures?

For me, the process of emptying my mental trash can was very humiliating and painful. Yet, for all the shame and pain that I suffered, I reaped rewards a thousand times over.

in the past. You know, clear up some issues that I had not gotten closure on and that had tainted my perception of myself.

Think about this for a minute. How can we really expect to be successful and feel a sense of fulfillment from either our lives or our careers when what we really feel deep down inside is remorse and guilt about things that we have done to others and ourselves?

> How can we really expect to be successful and feel a sense of fulfillment from either our lives or our careers when what we really feel deep down inside is remorse and guilt about ourselves and things that we have done?

I do not believe that we can. How many issues do you have to clear up? Until I dealt with all of my issues and put them into perspective, I felt like I would not be able to start over. What I learned by doing this was that other people, like yourself, may need to do what I have done.

One of the last issues that I identified and had to deal with when cleansing my consciousness and emptying my mental trash can concerned a good friend of mine, Don. Upon taking a position as Business Development Manager for a contractor in Atlanta some years ago, I quickly realized that I had to make some close relationships within the architectural community. The problem was that it was a very tightly woven organization. Funny, my dad was working for the same contractor and helped me get the job, as he had often helped me before.

Anyway, I don't remember exactly where or how, but I met a man named Don, who befriended me and took me under his wing. He spent a lot of time sharing what he knew with me and helping me to understand the obstacles that I would have to overcome in order to be successful in my new position. Over the course of a year or so, we grew to be, I think, more than just good friends. Don, our wives, and I shared a lot of time just talking about the things that were going on in each of our lives, me with my job and my wife, and he with his son and his business. Looking back now, I remember that he was one of my only friends at that time in my life. My wife and I viewed Don and his wife as confidants and as people who we could count on in a pinch. We hope they viewed us as the same.

As I'd done many times before, I left that job with the contractor for many reasons, mostly my own, and started my own marketing representative company, representing various firms from the health care community in Georgia. After all, I had made some good contacts, knew my way around, and could utilize the outstanding reputation of my father and myself to help me get in the door of places other people sometimes had problems with. That seemed like a good way to make a living at the time. Not!

Don agreed to let me represent his architectural company without hesitation. I think he allowed me to represent his firm because he wanted to help me out of a jam more than he wanted a marketing rep. But Don also knew that I was unhappy and unfulfilled. I pursued some clients for his firm for about a month or so, before taking yet another position with another company. As I'd done several times before, I ended up moving halfway across the country to take a new job. I remember I left in such a hurry that I did not even say thank you to his face for all of his help. I did make a phone call to him. That petty phone call was supposed to be my attempt to thank him for his help and for befriending my wife and me. What's worse, I did not have the courage to call him for almost two years after I moved, because I felt such a tremendous amount of guilt and anxiety over that situation. I did what I believe many of us would do in a similar situation, when we sort of screw a friend over. I hid my feelings regarding the issue and buried them deep inside. I thought it would not make that much difference to me in the long run, but it did.

Over time, these events and others like them produced overwhelming feelings of guilt and anxiety in me. These feelings on my conscience became overwhelming at times. I finally found the courage to deal with the situation and, as ashamed as I am right now to admit it, I saved the issue with Don as one of the last issues to be dealt with, because it was one of the biggest issues that I had to face.

Guess what? I picked up the phone the other day and I called him. Even more than I had hoped, he said that he was glad to hear from me and that he'd kept up with what and how my wife and I were doing through conversations with my dad, which blew me away. He still cared about my wife and me.

I told him my story and apologized as best I could over the telephone. It was a very emotional release for me to have simply picked up that telephone and made that phone call. Much to my surprise, he agreed to see me when I made my next trip to Georgia. I can't tell you in words what a relief it was just talking to him, much less his words to me during our conversation: "It's OK Joe, I forgive you. I'm just glad to hear from you, 'cause we've been worried about you."

Cleansing our consciousness and emptying our mental trash cans is not that hard to do, really. Many of the things that I had to do to empty my mental trash can were as simple as apologizing to someone for something that I had done. If the issue that I identified with was within myself or one more complicated, I may have had to think of another way to deal with it.

You see, negative events in life have a way of catching up to all of us. I believe that our mental trash cans get full in the first place because we have too many things going on: too much of everything that affects our ability to make rational decisions and get closure on things to allow us to act prudently.

You see, negative events in life have a way of catching up to all of us.

So, how do we clear our consciousness and empty our mental trash cans?

Step 1: Purchase or find a small trash can, or find one that you can use for a while to complete this process. Any regular old trash can will do fine. This will be your "mental trash can."

Step 2: Identify all of the things, people, or events that have ever caused you guilt, anxiety, or remorse and write each one of them down on a small, separate piece of paper. Make sure that you identify all of the issues, events, and people that have ever bothered you, even if you think they are insignificant.

Step 3: Crumble each piece into a ball and put them all into your mental trash can.

Step 4: Every day, take a piece of paper out of your mental trash can and read it. If it is an issue that you are ready to deal with and to get closure on, do so. If it is an issue that you are not ready to deal with, wad it back up and put it back in the trash can, then search for another one and work on it.

Step 5: After closing or resolving the issue that you decided to work on, close it for good.

Much of the reason that our mental trash cans get full in the first place is because we have too many things going on. They take a tremendous amount of our attention. They take too much of everything that affects our ability to make rational decisions and get closure on things.

This simple process allowed me to deal with each issue one at a time, rationally and without the influence of all the other things that were going on in my head. It simply takes the overwhelming part out of the process of emptying your mental trash can.

Most importantly, I learned how to face the issues of daily life, something that can be filled with anxiety and guilt.

Throw that piece of paper away forever. It should never bother you again!

Step 6: Continue this process each day until there are no more issues written on pieces of paper in your mental trash can. It's that simple.

Why does this work?

It is almost impossible to deal with all of the issues that make us feel emotions like guilt and anxiety all at once. Things get overwhelming. This simple process allowed me to deal with each issue one at a time, rationally and without the influence of all the other things going on in my head. It simply takes the overwhelming part out of the process of emptying your mental trash can. The entire process took only about one month to complete, but the rewards I have received far outweigh the small investment.

Today, I have a clear conscience. I have tried to make restitution for the actions that were holding me back, gravitating me to the past without allowing me to move on to the future. What I learned through this process will be valuable to me for the rest of my life. I learned how to cope, not mope. I learned how to make better decisions. I learned how to say: "I am sorry" to others, and mean it. I learned how to accept humiliation and how to be sincere. I learned how to value my friendships. Ultimately, I learned how to utilize a strategic psychological process to help me cope with life's unpleasant issues, issues that we all face from time to time. I learned how to face them without fear and one at a time. Most importantly, I learned how to face the issues of daily life.

CHAPTER 12

WE NEED A MISSION

A PURPOSE FOR OUR LIVES AND OUR CAREERS!

What's the purpose of your life and your career? Do you have a mission?

A mission gives us a sense of purpose—a reason to do what we do. Each of us wants to feel like what we are doing is important and that we have a higher purpose for doing what it is that we do. I know that I do. All of us also have things we feel we are supposed to be doing with our lives and our careers.

What are you supposed to be doing with your life and your career?

Here's a common problem: Too few of us ever follow our intuitions regarding what the purpose for our lives and careers really is. Consequently, we may muddle our way through a life and a career that has little or no meaning. Essentially, not defining your mission is actually a process of succumbing to mediocrity and your fears surrounding succeeding.

Most of my mistakes were made due to two simple reasons. One, my mission was one of a suicidal nature to start with; by suicidal I mean that my mission defied and violated many of the basic laws of success, such as helping

I judged my level of success by how much stuff I had in my garage, instead of how much love I had in my heart and how many friends I had. I was wrong.

other people. My previous mission was to make as much money as possible and to surround myself with material possessions. I judged my level of success by how much stuff I had in my garage, instead of how much love I had in my heart and how many friends I had. I was wrong. Does this sound familiar?

Second, I did not listen to my intuitions about what I knew was right and wrong regarding the way that I lived my life and pursued my career. In other words, I allowed other influences to make my decisions for me, which changed my mission.

A mission facilitates and clarifies the meaning of who we are and what it is that we do. It gives us our needed vision for success and provides us with a reason or a sense of purpose for continuing to do whatever it is that we do, even in the worst of conditions.

You see, a mission facilitates and clarifies the meaning of who we are and what it is that we do. It gives us our needed vision for success and provides us with a reason or a sense of purpose for continuing to do whatever it is that we do, even in the worst of conditions.

Without a mission to give us a sense of purpose to drive our beliefs, decisions, questions, and actions, it is easy to simply succumb to a life of mediocrity. Do not let this happen to you.

A MENTAL MISSION = ASPIRATION = INSPIRATION = DEDICATION = A DESTINATION!

With the creation of a mission, we quickly develop the commitment that is necessary to succeed, and we find an overwhelming sense of purpose in our lives that will motivate us to be successful.

Creating a mission for ourselves means that we have identified exactly what we want, and we have made a written plan of action that will guide us to a successful destination. With the creation of a mission, we quickly develop the commitment that is necessary to succeed, and we find an overwhelming sense of purpose in our lives that will motivate us to be successful. This feeling or sense of purpose enables us to continue to pursue success with a relentless passion in whatever we do; it feels good. If you have not defined a mission that will translate into a sense of purpose for your life and your career, do it NOW on a separate sheet of paper! Dedicate yourself to something that will motivate you to take action, and resolve not to give in to anything, anybody, or any of your fears.

Today, my mission is to pursue success by helping other people succeed in living a more fulfilled life and career. Whether I accomplish my mission through my own company or through some other means does not really matter. What matters is that I accomplish my mission. This is a mission that I am proud of. Helping other people is powerfully motivating in itself. What's your mission?

Helping other people is powerfully motivating in itself.

CHAPTER 13

UTILIZING OUR TRUE POTENTIAL FOR SUCCESS!

The tremendous number of people who waste their true talent and gifts in this world never ceases to amaze me. If we were only to live up to our true potential, we would be successful beyond belief.

If we were only to live up to our true potential, we would be successful beyond belief.

I've found that successful people simply utilize the natural talent with the most potential to help them achieve success. They maximize their potential by matching what they do well naturally with what they like to do.

Do you have a gift or talent that you intuitively feel, and that you really want to utilize? Is there one special talent and potential for success that you know you have but, for whatever reason, you cannot use? Why? One reason may be that you are afraid of what other people, like your family, spouse, and friends, will say. So rather than utilizing your special talent, you hide it, never tapping into what comes naturally to you. I understand that musicians experience this, so they often hide their talent due to the fear of what others would say if people knew they were a musician.

Or, maybe another reason is because you realize that in order to utilize this special talent, you will have to get some cooperation and support from the other people in your life, which you can't get. Do the other people in your life only dwell on the negative aspects of your idea to utilize your talent? Why? Here's the answer: because ultimately, they do not want the tremendous responsibility of helping you achieve your potential for success, unless it involves nothing more than a little guidance from them.

Guess what? By the time you realize what you want to do that utilizes your talent and potential for success, and you finally get the courage to try it regardless of what anyone says, you might be in too much debt to change careers. Don't wait! What do you do if you're buried in debt like most of us? My answer is that you find the courage to change your life today. Don't wait another minute! You may miss the opportunity to utilize your true potential for success by doing what comes natural to you.

Each of us is blessed at birth with some natural talent. Yes, even you! We're all gifted with something that we naturally do well, but too few of us use these talents and gifts to attract our own form of success. So we go through our lives and careers doing things that we do not like to do and can not naturally do well. Why do so many of us do that?

> Each of us is blessed at birth with some natural talent or something that we intuitively do well, but too few of us use these talents and gifts to attract our own form of success.

There are many reasons. One reason in particular is fear, fear of striking out on our own and doing what we really do well, regardless of what anyone says and thinks. Not utilizing our true potential in life leads to a lifetime of unanswered questions and continuous searching for something to fill the void, because we are not using our natural talents. Ultimately, depression and burnout are the last result, of not

> Not utilizing our true potential in life leads to a lifetime of unanswered questions and a continuous search for something to fill the void, because we are not using our natural talents.

Do you believe, like many of us, that you have a talent or gift that you have wasted?

I believe that failure to utilize our potential makes many of us unhappy with our work. Consequently, it's not hard to understand why so many people feel trapped in a job with no future.

Do you feel like you are wasting your talent and not utilizing your potential?

For whatever reason, most of us either do not get the support that we need from others to do what we'd like to do that will utilize our true potential, or we ignore using our talents because we are too afraid to try to do anything that may involve taking some risks in order to be successful.

utilizing natural talents, at least they were for me. Let me explain further.

Do you believe that you have a talent or gift that you have wasted?

When we do not utilize our potential and our talents, I believe that our minds and our bodies intuitively throw up roadblocks, like depression and anxiety, to let us know that we are miserable doing what we are doing; we need to change things. Consequently, I believe that this theory explains why most people "job-hop." You see, it's not the money that people seek in a new job; they are simply seeking an opportunity to utilize their natural potential and often hidden talents. Not utilizing their potential makes them unhappy with what they do for work. Sound familiar? It's not hard to understand why so many people feel trapped in a job with no future. Does any job today have a future?

Do you feel like you are wasting your time? Time that you could be spending doing something that you enjoy? I know these feelings all too well.

Try to understand this: It is never too late to try using your natural talents and gifts, even if you only utilize your potential and natural talents part time, or as a hobby.

Before I started my consulting firm, *Top of the Hill*, I wasted much of the natural talent that I was given at birth; it has taken me years to be able to live with it and do something about it. I was fortunate enough to have been gifted with three natural talents. Unfortunately, I have completely wasted and neglected two of them that I really love—music and athletics. Music, athleticism, and the gift of gab are my three natural talents. When I was a child, I could sing very well; I still can. I could easily play instruments I'd never played before. However, I was too young to intuit the value of these gifts. The same thing goes for my athletic talents. I was naturally stronger than many of the kids my age. As I grew older, I began to utilize some of this potential in high school athletics, but I never had the proper internal or external motivation to do anything with it. After bodybuilding for eight years and getting a lot of grief from my family for doing it, I quit, like a coward. I listened to other people tell me what to do, so, like a fool, I quit utilizing that particular true potential that I had to be an outstanding athlete. As for my gift of gab, I use that natural talent every day, because I am naturally a salesperson.

Do you intuit or feel like you have a particular talent or gift and you are not using it? Do you feel an insurmountable amount of stress and anxiety regarding the fact that you are not utilizing your true potential?

Today, I only dabble a little with my athletic and musical talents. I sing a bit of karaoke and write some music in my home studio and that's enough. With my training and development company, I am for the first time in my career actually utilizing one of my natural talents in order to succeed; and it feels good, really good.

My point in this chapter is **do not waste your natural talents**. I feel fortunate to have had the opportunity to still have a natural talent left to utilize after what I have been through in my life. I do frequently wonder how different my life would be had I chosen one of the other natural talents that I have and pursued one of them for a career. The answer? It came to me just now! Why have I been so blind? Maybe the universal laws of nature helped me choose my career path over the other options that I could have chosen because what I do today helps other people and that is where my true potential for success lies. I'd like to think that is the case.

Maybe I was not destined to sing or be a professional athlete. Maybe those talents were intended for me to have fun with, but my true potential lies in my ability to help other people. It is no coincidence that my life and my career have worked out the way that they have, and I like it!

Begin using your natural talents now. Do what comes naturally to you and you'll attract success. Find a way to utilize the things in which you have natural talents and potential for success, even if you start small and only use them for a hobby.

I have identified 12 natural talents that can exist in each of us and will actually attract success. Which one or ones do you intuitively identify with? Which has the most potential for you to become successful?

The 12 natural talents

1. Factual potential

2. Analytical potential

3. Linguistic potential

4. Spatial potential

5. Practical potential

6. Musical potential

7. Physical potential

8. Intuitive potential

9. Interpersonal potential

10. Theoretical potential

11. Comical potential

12. Supernatural potential

The 12 Natural Talents

1. **Factual potential**

2. **Analytical potential**

3. **Linguistic potential**

4. **Spatial potential**

5. **Practical potential**

6. **Musical potential**

7. **Physical potential**

8. **Intuitive potential**

9. **Interpersonal potential**

10. **Theoretical potential**

11. **Comical potential**

12. **Supernatural potential**

Is your career path based upon a utilization of your natural talents?

CHAPTER 14

THE POWER OF GIVING TO OTHERS AND LEAVING NARCISSISM BEHIND

How truly powerful giving to others and leaving narcissism behind can be! I've learned so much from doing this one, simple thing. Giving to others and learning how to leave narcissistic behavior behind has probably taught me more than any other lesson that I have learned.

What does *narcissism* mean? Who could be considered a narcissist?

According to *The Random House Dictionary*, narcissism is defined as:

1. inordinate absorption in oneself
2. erotic gratification derived from administration of one's own body

More commonly defined, "narcissists" only think about themselves, do nothing to help other people, and act only in their own best interests. Do you know someone who's a narcissist?

It has taken me a long time to realize that there truly is no excuse for narcissistic behavior, and being narcissistic and thinking of only myself makes becoming successful much more difficult. Narcissistic behavior is another thing that becomes a state of mind and turns into a way of life. It's a hard habit to break.

More times than not, the stories that we see and read are about successful people who have helped someone or some organization and are being thanked for their contribution.

Generally, when we see or read stories of highly successful people, the stories do not contain information about how someone took advantage of everyone to get to the top. That's what happens on your average TV show; it's not real life. More times than not, the stories that we see and read about are stories about how successful people have helped someone or some organization, and they are being thanked for their contribution.

Each of us has needs and wants, and as my friend Bill says, "You gotta put your needs before your wants." Being needed, and having a feeling of being needed, is a basic requirement of our psyche. Sometimes we do not get enough of this stimulus in our lives. I've found it to be as true as true can be, and empowering, that there is a special feeling that we can receive as a result of giving to others. Coming from a person who rarely thought of anyone but himself, I should know.

BEGINNING THE PROCESS

What I've found to be as true as true can be, and even empowering, is that there is a positive feeling of power that I receive as a result of giving to others.

When I began to help my friends and family, I saw an increase in my own self-esteem as well as theirs, which was powerful. That was a step in the right direction. But sometimes friends and family can be the hardest people to help. Sometimes they don't want our help. If that's your situation, that's fine. Keep in mind, there are plenty of other people who need your help. However, I made significant progress after I began to help strangers—you know, everybody else. That's when I began to feel the power of being a giver instead of a taker. It changed me for the better, forever. That's why I began my career in the business of helping others.

"If life isn't giving to you, you aren't giving enough to it. The more you give, the more it gives back to you. This is a law of life."

—*Dr. Norman Vincent Peale*

When we only help ourselves, our friends, or our family members, we expect to get compliments and a feeling of satisfaction for being a giver and helping out. However, strangers or people that you hardly know generally don't freely give out compliments or thanks to anyone, even if you do help them. Receiving feelings of gratification and getting a simple "thank you" for helping people has to be earned through a genuine showing of your generosity, your compassion, and your willingness to help them. That's what makes giving to others so powerful.

I read a statement made by a man named Zig Ziglar. I want you to read it carefully, because it summarizes this chapter to a "T." I'm sure that you have heard of Zig. If not, he's one of the most respected names in the self-development business and you should read his work too. That statement is as follows: "You can get everything in life you want, if you help enough other people get what they want." (*Personal Selling Power* magazine, Anniversary Issue, p. 103.) That is among the truest of statements that I have ever read, and it makes perfect sense. It's such a perfect statement that I won't expand on it.

Here's a big question for you to think about. If you could choose any individual or any organization and donate to them some of your time and expertise, who would it be? Whoever you decide to help, you must remember that making a commitment to be a giver and to helping others is not something that you do only once.

"If life isn't giving to you, you aren't giving enough to it. The more you give, the more it gives back to you. This is a law of life."
—*Dr. Norman Vincent Peale*

Each of us needs and wants to be needed, and as my friend Bill says: "You gotta put your needs before your wants."

Receiving a feeling of gratification and a compliment from helping people has to be earned through a genuine showing of your generosity, your compassion, and your willingness to help. That's what makes giving to others so powerful.

"You can get everything in life you want, if you help enough other people get what they want."
—*Zig Ziglar*
This is among the truest of statements that I have ever read, and it makes perfect sense.

Like many other strategies that make us successful, helping other people and leaving narcissism behind takes a commitment to helping and giving to others for the rest of your life, not for just a couple of days.

If you could choose any individual or any organization and donate to them some of your time and expertise, who would it be?

Here are some examples of people or organizations that you might *volunteer* to help: your local hospital, family members, the local animal shelter, friends, neighbors, The Salvation Army, and the Red Cross, to name just a few. By the way, did you notice the word *volunteer* in the previous sentence? No payment allowed for your help!

The subject of helping others brings to mind an event that happened to me. I want to tell you about it. See if you can relate. Recently, I was fortunate enough to have conducted a "Managerial Characteristics" seminar for the Georgia Society of Healthcare Engineers, of which I am very proud. I appeared as a speaker at their quarterly meeting. I enlisted the help of my best friend Nick to tag along and help me out with the details. He agreed to go along and help me as he's done a hundred times before. He never asks for anything in return. Anyway, Nick and I flew from Kentucky to Atlanta, then rented a car and drove the rest of the way to our destination.

I made significant progress after I began to help strangers; you know, everybody else. That's when I began to intuitively feel the power of being a giver instead of a taker, and it changed me for the better.

Just being at the pre-meeting gave me an opportunity to say hello to a great number of old friends, which I enjoyed. The Georgia Society of Healthcare Engineers and friends was the same group that I was selling hospital construction services to just a few years ago.

It was an exciting time for me. Can you imagine it? There I was, surrounded by some of the people my father and I had known for years and they really wanted to hear what I had to say. In addition to providing them with a seminar, I hope I was able to rekindle some relationships that I value very much within that group.

Over the course of the weekend, Nick and I played a little golf (at which I stink). We smoked some good cigars and spent some quality time with one another. As usual, there was too much fun had by all and not enough rest. By the end of the seminar and weekend, we were both exhausted. We'd had enough fun, so we headed back to Atlanta to recharge our batteries and spend a night out on the town before leaving for home.

Upon arriving in Atlanta, my sister called me to ask if Nick, my dad, and I would help her do something. It was what she called at the time "a little help with a few things." She had recently completed a divorce and had to clear out the last of the items that she had split with her ex-husband. I distinctly remember hearing her say, "It shouldn't take long; there's not that much left." So Nick and I were enlisted in the moving army while my dad and my sister were, of course, the colonels of the operation. Who do you think got to supervise the entire operation? It certainly was not Nick or me.

Well, we all agreed to help her, but I told her that Nick and I had plans to go to Dave and Busters (a popular Atlanta fun spot), then on to Buckhead (another Atlanta fun spot) for the night. She said, "No problem, you'll be done in plenty of time." After all, Nick and I could not be that close to some of the hottest night spots in Atlanta and not go, now, could we? Of course not. Nick and I had planned to go out on the town since we first planned the trip. We were going no matter what.

The next day, Nick and I got up, "eased" (southern slang) on over to the moving van place, and rented a van to haul my sister's junk. We were not worried about missing out on our fun that night until my dad came out with the keys to the biggest van that the place had. I looked at Nick, then he looked at me and we both said, "Oh—!"

I said, "I knew it; we've been had." That's when Nick and I knew that we were probably going to be working all day. What else would my dad have gotten the biggest truck in the parking lot for, unless my sister had a ton of junk to put in it?

Later that day, we pulled up into the driveway, where we met my sister. She looked like she had been crying. That's when she said, "There may be a little more than I thought." Of course there was more than she thought. I had a feeling that there was going to be a lot of stuff to load when I saw the size of the truck. Should I have expected anything less than a whole house full of stuff from her? To top it off she quietly informed us that we had to do some other chores before we were done.

For a moment, after she told us all these interesting tidbits of information, I almost told her to kiss off and to do it herself instead of ruining *our* plans. In the past, I would have done just that. Instead, Nick and I looked at each other and said, "Whatever you need us to do, we will do it. We'll load up the whole place if that's what you need." She started to cry again. As I tried to comfort her, I told her that we were there to help, and not to worry, we would get it all done for her. However, I did start to complain about 9:00 that night, when I began to get hungry.

So, what's my point with this story? I did not have to help my sister move. But she had helped me through tougher times than simply moving. I know of many people who would have made up excuses as to why they could not help out. I know of some others that were supposed to help us that did just that. They may have told her to "pay somebody to do it," or "do it yourself, you never help me," or "I don't have time." I would have made those same excuses myself not that long ago. But you know what? Helping her made each of us, me, my dad, and Nick, feel good about ourselves. Imagine that. I helped someone and it made me feel good.

What would you have done in the same situation? Would you have helped, or would you have told her to kiss off?

This single incident and the events that surround it may seem trivial to you, but they helped my relationship with my sister and taught me a valuable lesson that I'd forgotten. After 29 years on the planet, I finally got the message of Zig's quote earlier in this chapter.

Well, as for moving her junk? It was a hard ten or twelve hours of work that really gave me a great feeling of knowing that I'd come to my sister's rescue when she needed me and that I did not let her down. With regards to narcissism? I've left the narcissism behind! My life is dedicated to helping others.

Try this to learn how to give to others and leave narcissism behind.

1. Begin by admitting that you may be narcissistic in your behavior and that you think of other people less than you should.

2. Volunteer to help someone (it does not really matter who) for two to three hours per week, every week for three months. Do not accept any payment for the help that you provide.

3. Designate ten minutes of every day to spend thinking about all of the other people that you know and something that you can do to help one or more of them.

Try doing this for just one week. If you will spend only ten minutes out of each of your days thinking of other people, you'll quickly begin to understand how powerful this strategy really is. Amazing things can happen as a result of leaving narcissism behind.

CHAPTER 15

THE POWER OF SILENCE

UNCONTROLLED-YET-CONTROLLED FOCUS

Many times I've enlisted "the power of silence" to help me collect my thoughts and to refocus my energy. Have you?

I think I began to use the power of silence when I was a kid. I grew up in Atlanta on the Chattahoochee River, fishing as much as I could. Being the loner that I was, I became consciously aware of how truly powerful silence can be when it is utilized on a regular basis. I used to love lying down by the river, just listening and thinking.

Like many of the strategies in this book, learning how to use silence itself takes practice. You have to do more than just turn off the TV and lie down on the couch for a nap. You have to relax and let your mind wander. That can be hard to do when the TV is on, or if you are being distracted. When we allow the racing thoughts of the day to subside and let our minds wander, we have the ability to open up our creativity and stimulate the new ideas that have been put aside while we go about our daily routines.

For most of us, we have all that we can do to remain focused on each day's tasks at hand.

Review & Quotes & for Your Notes

Many times I've enlisted **The Power Of Silence** to help me collect my thoughts and to refocus my energy. Have you?

Like many of the strategies in this book, learning how to use silence takes practice.

How much of our time is spent in an "uncontrolled-yet-controlled focus" state of mind just completely relaxing and thinking?

When we utilize "Uncontrolled-Yet-Controlled Focus," we can experience totally different and new thoughts or ideas. It's these new ideas that can make us successful.

With everything we have going on in our lives, it is easy for our conscious mind to suppress or hide what the unconscious mind holds deep inside. It's been said that our most advanced ideas and creativity are found in the subconscious mind.

Silently allowing our minds to wander, or uncontrollably-yet-controllably focus, is one way to get to the thoughts in our subconscious minds and increase our potential to harness the ideas that constitute success.

The reason why uncontrolled-yet-controlled focus is such a powerful strategy is because it opens up a new thinking process to most of us, and allows us to tap into our subconscious. When we utilize "Uncontrolled-Yet-Controlled Focus," we can experience totally different and new thoughts or ideas. It's these new ideas that can make us successful.

You see, what happens is quite simple. With everything we have going on in our lives, it is easy for our conscious mind to suppress or hide what the unconscious mind holds deep inside. It's been said that our most advanced ideas and creativity are found in the subconscious mind. That being true, silently allowing our minds to wander, or uncontrollably-yet-controllably focus, is one way to get to the thoughts in our subconscious minds and increase our potential to harness the ideas that contribute to our success.

Here's how I used The Power Of Silence and Uncontrolled-Yet-Controlled Focus to change my life; try it for yourself before you dismiss this strategy as hogwash:

When I am ready, I find a quiet place and get comfortable. I allot a half hour of my day, usually two days per week; and I make sure that I bring either my tape recorder or a pad and pencil to write any interesting thoughts or ideas down, so I will not forget them when they enter my mind. When I feel comfortable, I close my eyes and let the excitement of the day slowly pass; I begin simply to let my mind wander until I think of an interesting idea or topic. I let any and all thoughts freely enter my mind.

For me, the thinking process usually begins with thoughts of the day, things that I don't want to forget. After quickly recapping the day, I drift into more interesting thoughts and subjects, with more in-depth meaning to them. When I come across an interesting idea, I either write it down or verbally acknowledge it on tape. Then, I either expand my thoughts on the subject, or I move on to something else, some other idea. Sometimes I think of many new things; sometimes I drift off into a relaxing nap, which is sometimes good, too, but is the not goal of the therapy. This process, I believe, increases our ability to tap the subconscious mind, which results in simply thinking more clearly, effectively, and creatively.

Anyway, try it for yourself and decide whether this strategy works for you before you dismiss it as being silly. It has made a noticeable difference in my life.

CHAPTER 16

THE LAWS OF SUCCESS

**Review & Quotes
& for Your Notes**

We live in a world where nature's laws prevail every day. There is also an unspoken set of success laws. Properly aligning ourselves with these laws and adhering to them will increase our probability of success. However, violating the laws of success will push us farther away from success.

SUCCESS LAW #1
You can create a controlled obsession, a burning desire to reach your goals and dreams, providing you find balance.

SUCCESS LAW #2
You must be dedicated to helping other people and leaving your narcissistic behavior behind.

SUCCESS LAW #3
You must make good decisions.

SUCCESS LAW #4
You must learn how to plan and perform actions for your success day by day.

Michael Korda, author of *Success*, wrote: "Judge your performance by what you have done *today*, not what you did yesterday or what you plan to do tomorrow."

SUCCESS LAW #5

You do not have to do a job that you hate.

Your chances of achieving success are better if you love or at least tolerate your work.

SUCCESS LAW #6
You must learn from your mistakes.

Successful people make mistakes, but rarely make the same mistake twice!

SUCCESS LAW #7
You must assume ultimate responsibility for your successes, failures, and obligations.

SUCCESS LAW #8
Clear your consciousness and relieve your guilt.

Make amends with everyone. You can't feel guilty and embark on a journey for success.

SUCCESS LAW #9
You must finish what you start! If you can't finish what you start, don't start it.

SUCCESS LAW #10
Regularly cycle energy through your mind, your spirit, and your body. It's what we do naturally.

SUCCESS LAW #11
Eat successfully. Avoid the "after-lunch sleepies" by eating light lunches.

SUCCESS LAW #12
Learn and practice virtues like self-control.

SUCCESS LAW #13
Lower your expectations of others.

Michael Korda, regarding successful people: "They never underestimate other people's innate ability to make trouble, and allow for this factor in all their plans."

CHAPTER 17

TAKING ON THE
ULTIMATE RESPONSIBILITY

**Review & Quotes
& for Your Notes**

You alone control your
destiny, unless you allow
other people control
it for you by making the
decisions that affect your
life and your career.

You alone control your destiny, unless other people control it for you by making the decisions that affect your life and your career.

Let's assume for a minute that you can't seem to make a relationship work, or maybe you just can't seem to make a job work as you'd like it to. Whose responsibility is it to make these things work? The answer? It's your responsibility—no one else's. If you have not done so yet, it's time to take complete control of your life, and taking on the ultimate responsibility is the way to start.

Let's assume for a
minute that you can't
seem to make a
relationship work,
or maybe you just
can't seem to make
a job work as
you'd like it to.
Whose responsibility
is it to make
these things work?

If you agree with me that it's time to truly take control of your career and your life, then you will accept the ultimate responsibility for whether or not you become successful. Nothing that we do in life "just happens," except *nothing*. We make things happen by either doing something or by doing nothing. If you are wondering why you are not as successful as you should be, ask yourself if you're playing "the blaming game."

What's the blaming game? That's the game that we play when we blame everybody but ourselves for our mistakes and for the things that happen to us, or in most cases that don't happen to us. Think about this: The last time you experienced a failure or made a mistake, either large or small, did you place the blame on someone else? It has become a very common procedure in today's society, and it's wrong.

Many of us blame everyone but ourselves when things don't go right. It's easier just to blame someone else than to accept the responsibility for our actions and our decisions.

Let's look at an example of how *not* taking the ultimate responsibility works, and let's get an understanding of *why* it does not work. Assume for a minute that you are a mid-level manager at your company. Your boss wants a report done and he wants it on his desk by 10:00 AM tomorrow. Now, you have written the report and have turned it in to an assistant that you hired to type it for you. Then, you give the assistant explicit instructions to have the report done by 9:00, so you can proofread it and make any last-minute changes before turning it in to your boss. The next day, it's 9:55 and you don't have a copy of the report; when you do finally get a copy, it is botched beyond repair. You realize that there is no time to retype the report. It's now 10:00 o'clock, the meeting has begun, and you begin explaining to your boss why the report is not ready. What are you going to say and do? Are you going to blame the botched report on your assistant, or will you take the responsibility for the report being botched and late? Whose responsibility was it to have the report done on time anyway?

Here's the answer: Ultimately, it was your responsibility to see that the report was done

Nothing that we do in life "just happens," except *nothing*.

We make things happen by doing something or, in some cases, by doing nothing.

If you are wondering why you are not as successful as you should be, ask yourself if you're playing "the blaming game."

The last time you experienced a failure or made a mistake, either large or small, did you place the blame on someone else?

Many of us blame everyone but ourselves when things don't go right or do not go our way, because it's easier to just blame someone else than to accept responsibility for our actions and our decisions.

on time. The fact that the report is not finished is ultimately not your assistant's responsibility. Ultimately, it's your responsibility. Here's why: In this scenario, you hired an assistant who does lousy work; that's your responsibility. You allowed the report to be late. You did not follow up with your assistant to make sure that the report was done properly. You did not allow enough time for mistakes. You agreed to have the report on your boss' desk at 10:00; it's your responsibility to do so, **no matter what!**

You see, the report would not have been late if you had taken on the ultimate responsibility for having such an important report done well and on time. Whether you delegated the job to someone else or not is not the issue. The issue is that you, and no one else, agreed to have the report on the boss's desk at 10:00, and it did not happen. Consequently, who do you think will *not* get that promotion that's coming up? You! Who has risked their job and made themselves look like a rookie? You did.

Here's a tip. Double check everything when it's your butt on the line!

Here is an example of a blaming game of my own. When I was selling health care construction in Atlanta, I had trouble for quite some time understanding whose responsibility it was for winning or losing a project. I could not understand why we were losing bids to companies not nearly as good as we were. Sure, there were differences in our bidded dollar amounts, but other firms that were not the low bidder were winning bids on jobs. Why weren't we winning project bids?

When I began with the company, my position was Healthcare Business Development Manager, which really meant glorified salesperson. I was told that my job was to secure the relationships necessary for us either to submit bids or to negotiate contracts with key personnel throughout Georgia's hospital, engineering, and architectural communities. Then I would turn the project over to our in-house estimators and other personnel within the company to complete the bidding process. It sounded simple enough in the beginning.

Throughout my employment we lost several projects; I tried to find the reason why, so we would not make the same mistakes twice. In the beginning, it was easy to find fault with everyone but myself. Placing the blame for a project loss on anybody but myself was how I covered up my own mistakes and pushed my responsibilities off on someone else. I remember thinking to myself, "I did my part; I did what I was told to, but someone else screwed up the project, that's why we lost it."

> When you do accept the ultimate responsibility, you will see how much the responsibility for you becoming successful or not really is your own.

However, after closer examination, I realized that ultimately it was my responsibility to win or lose those projects, no one else's. It was my responsibility to create the relationships that I needed with my clients in order to be successful. It was my responsibility to create strong relationships inside the company with the people working on the projects I had secured for bid; and it was my responsibility to ask of them their best work, which I forgot to do until it was too late. Win, lose, or draw, it was my responsibility because no matter who screwed what up, or who did their job well, winning was how I was making my living. I was paid to take on the responsibility for the successes and the failures of my division of the company.

When I finally realized all of this, I began taking steps to increase my involvement and contribution to the process of winning or losing projects. I must have stepped on a few toes along the way, because the office politics that I encountered became more than I was willing to put up with. My efforts to do good were too little, too late. I'd already done some damage from within the company, and I remember the process being more like "damage repair" than creating relationships.

So when I decided that the office politics and the odds in making the situation better were, at the time, more than I was willing to try to overcome, I left that company. I left that company for the wrong reasons. Oh well.

If you are wondering why you are not as successful as you can be, try analyzing your situation, and try to determine whether or not you are accepting the ultimate responsibility for your successes and failures. When you do accept the ultimate responsibility, you will see how much the responsibility for you becoming successful or not really is your own.

If you are wondering why you are not as successful as you can be, try analyzing your situation, and try to determine whether or not you are accepting the ultimate responsibility for your successes and failures.

CHAPTER 18

MAKING BETTER DECISIONS WITH A COMMITMENT FOR SUCCESS!

Decisions, decisions, decisions. To become more successful, we have to learn how to make better decisions. The question is: How do we make better decisions?

Much of my life was spent making the wrong decisions, and making them for the wrong reasons. I did not know how to make decisions, and as a result I sometimes lost my motivation to pursue success in the confusion of everyday life.

Do you make the right decisions? Do you leave your decisions to chance, circumstance, or consequence?

Like everything else, making good decisions takes practice. Many of us have come to rely too much on other people's input and not on our own intuitions regarding what we feel is right or wrong, what is good or bad for us when making decisions. Consequently, we make decisions that are right for someone other than ourselves; we do not make good decisions because we are afraid of making the wrong decision. So we allow other people to make them for us. Doing this gives us something

Review & Quotes & for Your Notes

In order for us to become more successful, we have to learn how to make better decisions.

other than ourselves to place the blame upon if we fail to make a good decision. However, once you accept the ultimate responsibility for your successes, failures, and decisions, you have made one of the most important and significant decisions that you will ever make. Even though all of your decisions might not be right ones, you will still have made a decision to control your own life and career, a decision that will ultimately lead you to be a more healthy, successful, and fulfilled individual.

I want you to think very hard about this next statement: It is at the moment that a decision is made to do something and take action toward our dreams and goals that we will begin to see some noticeable results. You see, until you make a decision to do something, you are only talking, thinking, hoping, wishing, or dreaming about taking the necessary actions to become successful. A decision to do something, to take action, makes achieving our dreams and goals, as well as succeeding, a real possibility.

Utilizing the process of INTUITIVE CONSCIOUSNESS described in chapter 8, which requires us to listen to our intuitions and conscious thoughts, we can make better decisions concerning our happiness and the happiness of those around us.

Our accomplishments and level of success in life are measured by our decisions to do something. The decisions that we make to do the things that we do, not to talk about them, make us successful. Have you ever known anyone who is successful that did not make good decisions, that did not make a decision to take some action and do something? Even a person who may have done nothing all their life, who ended up winning the lottery and became rich, first made the decision to buy a lottery ticket.

Even if we make a decision to do nothing, we still have made a decision to do something.

When I began to make my own decisions I was finally able to take control of my own life and career. I had made a habit of either asking other people for their advice or simply not making a decision at all. I was, however, good at talking about doing things, just not actually doing them. I fully understood the value of making my own decisions when I decided to leave my employer in South Dakota and start my consulting/training company *Top of the Hill.* At the moment I made the decision to leave and strike out on my own, I took my fate into my own hands, and out of the hands of others. At the time, whether I became successful or not made no significant difference to me. What made a difference to me, and what changed my life forever, was the fact that I had found the internal courage to make the decision on my own. It felt good to make a decision to do something on my own.

> I did not know how to make decisions, and as a result I sometimes lost my motivation to pursue success in the confusion of everyday life.

Another example is the decision that I made to write this book. Then and only then, when the decision was made to sit down and write, did the possibility of writing this book become real. If I had not made the simple decision to sit my fanny down and write the book, I'd still be just hoping, wishing, thinking, dreaming, or talking about writing it.

This next point is interesting: Our search for enough facts to make our decisions properly adds to the difficult task of decision making. Many times, we will not make a decision simply because we do not have enough facts. One thing I have learned through experience is that no amount of facts can replace intuition and feelings. More often than not, our intuitions are right. Follow your intuitions, and use the facts as a buffer when making your decisions. It's when we do not follow our intuitions and our consciousness and rely solely on the facts that we make our mistakes.

> Do you make the right decisions? Do you leave your decisions to chance? To circumstance? To consequence?

"Facts are a decision-maker's tools, but (1) they won't take the place of intuition, (2) they won't make the decision for you, and (3) they are only as useful as your ability to interpret them."
—Mark H. McCormack, What They Don't Teach You at Harvard Business School

When we try to make our decisions, many of us have come to rely too much on other people's input, and not our own intuitions regarding what we feel is right or wrong, good or bad. Consequently, we make decisions that are right for someone other than ourselves.

Even though all of your decisions might not be right ones, you still will have made a decision to control your own life and your career, which will ultimately lead you to be a more healthy, successful, and fulfilled individual.

"Facts are a decision-maker's tools, but (1) they won't take the place of intuition, (2) they won't make the decision for you, and (3) they are only as useful as your ability to interpret them."
—Mark H. McCormack,
What They Don't Teach You at Harvard Business School (p.232)

Regarding decisions? Make no mistake. If you do not make your own life and career decisions, they will be made for you. If you have not made a career decision regarding what you really want to do for work, at some point, out of the necessity for money to live on, the system in which we live will make the decision for you. Unless you either steal the money or you are rich enough not have to work for a living, you will have to get a job doing something in order to exist on this planet. In this scenario, you will probably be forced to take on a job that you are not happy with. So many of us have not made critical decisions regarding our career and lives for our own happiness. Here's what typically happens: We get stuck with a life or a career that we hate. Then we complain about it. How stupid is that? Pretty stupid.

So, how do we make decisions that are right for us?

The answer to this question lies within you. What do you need in order to feel comfortable making your own decisions? Do you have the courage to make your own decisions? Do you allow others to influence your decisions? Do you accept the ultimate responsibility for your good and bad decisions?

Here's how I make my really tough decisions. Take what you learn from my process and use it to help you make your decisions.

1. I think about the decision that I need to make by listening to my intuitions and my conscious thoughts.

2. I take time to Intuitively and Consciously understand what the positive and the negative effects of the decision will be.

3. I ask myself, "What is the worst thing that could happen as a result of the decision I am about to make?" and "What's the best thing that can happen?"

4. I determine what the consequences are and whether or not the benefits outweigh the negative effects of the decision.

5. If I must, I consult with others in order to get more information.

6. I put my fear of making the decision to rest by accepting the responsibility for making either a good or a bad decision.

7. I then make the decision that I have to make, and I stick to it.

Once a decision is made, make a commitment to your decision!

Have you ever made a decision to "do something" and then for some reason not followed it through by doing what you'd decided to do?

Sure. We all have. It is easy enough to make decisions. But what I've found to be difficult is following through on our tougher decisions. Well, I've discovered a simple remedy for these situations when we have made a decision, but we lack the necessary commitment to follow through. It's called the Written and Witnessed Commitment, or contract for action. Here's how it works:

It is at the moment that a decision is made to do something, to take action toward our dreams and goals, that we will begin to see some noticeable results.

You see, until you make a decision to do something, you are only talking, thinking, hoping, wishing, or dreaming about taking the necessary actions for you to become successful and live out your dreams and goals.

Our accomplishments and level of success in life are measured by our decisions to do something.

It's the decisions that we make to do things, not just to talk about doing them, that make us successful.

Until a decision is made, we cannot take intuitively questioned and evaluated action on our beliefs.

Even if we make a decision to do nothing, we still have made a decision to do something.

I believe it to be true that no amount of facts can replace the intuition or feeling that can help us to make a decision.

Our search for "enough facts" adds to the difficult task of decision making.

Follow your intuitions, and use the facts as a buffer when making your decisions. It's when we do not follow our intuitions and our consciousness, when we rely solely on the facts, that we make our mistakes.

Make no mistake. If you do not make your own life and career decisions, they will be made for you.

If you are one of those people that is continually complaining about your life or your career, and you're not happy, keep reading this book and change things today or shut up!

The Written and Witnessed Commitment

After you make your decision to do whatever it is you've decided, draw up a simple written and witnessed commitment, or contract for action, with the person or group of people that you value the most. Examples of these are spouses, children, coworker or coworkers, etc. Next, describe in the contract exactly what the decision that you have made is.

"I've made the decision to _____."

Next, describe exactly what action you will have to take in order to follow through on the decision.

"I will have to _____."

Next, specify a time and date for the completion of the actions, the things that you have to do surrounding your decision.

"I will complete this action on or before _____."

Finally, sign the contract and ask the person or group of people that you value the most to witness and sign the contract for you.

What the written and witnessed commitment does is simple. It demonstrates to your witness or witnesses that you are serious about upholding your commitment, and you need their help in order to help you do so. You and your witness or witnesses will feel obligated to uphold your commitment. You see, now you have shown yourself and your witness that you are absolutely committed to doing what you say; if either you or your witness do not follow through on the contract until the action is completed, you will have to look each other in the eye and admit to failing to uphold that commitment. Neither of you will want to do that. My

studies show that written and witnessed contracts are more than 76% likely to get followed
through than a decision to do something
made alone.

I learned the true value of the written and witnessed commitment or contract for action several years ago when I asked my friend Rich to
help me quit smoking. Here's the story: Rich
and I had been working in my tiny home office,
doing whatever. Anyway, I remember that it was
about 11:00 AM, and I'd already smoked about
three-quarters of a pack of cigarettes. The office
in which we worked was really small. So the
smoke made a sort of big, gray cloud that hung
around for hours. Being a veteran smoker of 21
years, I kinda liked it.

Suddenly, Rich turned to me and got my attention. His eyes were red and bloodshot. He looked
at me, squinted his eyes, and said, "I wish you
would quit smoking in here. It is giving me a
headache, and my eyes are burning."

I of course said something like, "Oh, it's good for
you," and went about my business. Smoking
had become such an acceptable habit for me
that I'd forgotten how much it might have been
negatively affecting Rich.

Next, he said, "I don't know why you smoke; it is
so stupid."

At that moment, I said, "Yeah, it is, isn't it?" I
remember sitting back in my chair for a minute
while I thought. I thought about it for a couple
of minutes, before making a decision to quit
smoking cigarettes forever.

I then turned to Rich and said, "You are right,
smoking these things is stupid, and I am
going to quit right now. We'll use my strategy

Have you ever made
a decision do "do
something" and then,
for whatever reason,
you did not follow
it through?

for success, the written and witnessed commitment."

Rich said, "What's that?"

I said, "Will you help me?"

Rich said, "I'll help you any way I can."

I quickly described the "written and witnessed commitment," or "contract for action," idea to him. He thought it was pretty neat. I drew up the contract on which I wrote these simple words: "I will quit smoking cigarettes today—Now! J.B.H." We both signed the contract, and each of us kept a copy. I will keep that contract with me for the rest of my life.

The moment that I signed that contract to quit smoking was the moment that I finally quit smoking, after 21+ years. The instant that we signed that contract, Rich and I were both obligated by more than just our word to do what we said we'd do; me to stop smoking, and he to help me quit. If I would not have quit, and if he had not helped me, not only would I have to look myself in the mirror, but I would have had to look Rich in the eye and wonder what he thought of me, as well. Every time that I wanted a cigarette, rather than allowing me to welch on my word, Rich held me to the contract with his words of encouragement. The contract made the whole process of quitting more meaningful, more important to both of us. I may have never been able to quit smoking without the written and witnessed contract for action and Rich's help.

Try using the Written and Witnessed Commitment for yourself. You'll soon see how truly effective this simple strategy really is.

CHAPTER 19

PLANNING OUR GOALS
AND DREAMS FOR SUCCESS

Life and a career—168 credit hours per week; you'll need a syllabus!

Why is it we spend so much time trying to succeed, and no time preparing to succeed? Why do we plan for success and material possessions instead of planning for fulfillment and happiness?

Life and a career—
168 credit hours
per week; you'll need
a syllabus!

We must plan our dreams and our goals for success. Plan our dreams and goals for success? What are goals? What are dreams? What's a plan? "The fact is, that only one goal in life makes sense. Fortunately, it's a goal within the reach of all of us. That goal is to seek the best life attainable in the here and now of our everyday existence" (Joseph Klock).

Many of us, as have I, "wing it" in our lives and in our careers. We have no real plans for what we want or how we will get it. We spend our time hoping, wishing, and dreaming about becoming successful and happy. I cannot convey how important having a plan really is. I know, most of us have a hard enough time planning our next day, much less our lives and our careers. However, creating a detailed plan of action for

Why is it we spend
so much time trying
to succeed, and no time
preparing ourselves
to succeed?

> "Only one goal in life makes sense. Fortunately, it's a goal within the reach of all of us. That goal is to seek the best life attainable in the here and now of our everyday existence."
> —Joseph Klock

> Trying to achieve success, happiness, and long-term fulfillment are things that are too important to just "wing it." Creating a detailed plan of action for our lives and our careers simply has to be done.

> Many of us lack the clarity in our lives and our careers that a plan can give.

> If I did not create a detailed plan of action to follow, I was destined to continue down the same marginally successful path that I had been following, never reaching my full potential in either my life or my career. I was destined to get only as far as my short-term thinking and planning would allow me to go, no further.

your life's happiness and your career success simply has to be done. Many of us lack the clarity in our lives and our careers that a plan can give. We seem to just do whatever that we have to do in order to exist and pay our bills. After all, that alone is tough enough for some of us. Nobody told me twenty years ago I had to plan out my life and my career goals and dreams. I thought I could become successful without creating a plan to follow, but I could not. I failed more times than I should have, simply because I lacked a detailed plan of action.

I realized that when I did identify my goals and dreams for my life and my career, such as being a successful athlete, owning my own company, writing books, and pursuing an extraordinary life and career, the goals and dreams that I had identified were pretty substantial ones, at times even overwhelming. I knew then that successfully achieving my dreams and goals would require a commitment to both a short- and long-term plan of action.

I was going to get what I wanted; I had to make a detailed plan for WHO I wanted to be, WHAT I wanted out of my life and my career, WHERE all of this would take place, WHEN each of my goals and dreams would become a reality, HOW I was going to make my dreams and goals come true, WHO I needed to help, and WHO would have to help me in order for me to succeed in achieving my goals and dreams. I came to the conclusion that I could no longer wing it.

I discovered through experience that if I did not create a detailed plan of action to follow, I was destined to continue down the same marginally successful path that I had been following, never reaching my full potential in either my life or my career. I was destined to get only as far as my short-term thinking and planning would allow me to go, no further. Sound familiar?

Consider this analogy: like a ship's captain plans and charts out a course for his voyage, we too must plan and chart out a course for our lives and our careers. A PLAN is how you get CLARITY and POWER into your life, the power and clarity to control your own destiny. Imagine that. You can control your own destiny. That alone is powerful. You are powerful!

So, exactly what are dreams, goals, and a plan?

Dreams are those things that we wish for, but which *seem* to be out of our reach. Most of us never really take any action to achieve them, other than idle wishes and hopes that a miracle will happen to make our dreams come true. Dreams are achievable through the use of a plan. Goals are those things that we identify as achievable or possible and of which we feel sufficiently confident of our ability to actually try and achieve. Goals are those things that we are willing to pursue and to sacrifice for. A plan is a written document that contains our dreams and our goals. It identifies exactly who we want to be, where our dreams and goals will take place, and when our dreams and goals will become a reality or completed. It identifies the people whose help we will need and those who will need our help, all in order for our dreams and goals to be achieved.

Highly successful, motivated, and happy people can break down a sometimes overwhelming dream of becoming successful into many smaller and achievable goals with the help of a plan. They write down their dream, break it down into achievable and smaller goals, then

Pursuing a successful life and career without a plan is essentially nothing more than thinking and living in terms of the short term only.

A PLAN is how you get CLARITY and POWER into your life, the power and clarity to control your own destiny.

Dreams are those things that we wish for, but which *seem* to be out of our reach.

Goals are those things that we identify as achievable or possible.

A plan is a written document that contains our dreams and our goals

Highly successful, motivated, and happy people simply break down a sometimes overwhelming dream into many smaller and achievable goals with the help of a plan.

A plan simply makes
life easier and
success possible.

formulate a plan of action to help them achieve each goal, one at a time, until their dream is achieved. Pretty simple, huh?

Success

Goals

Dreams

PLAN OF ACTION = SUCCESS

One dream of mine was to move to the beach, buy a big boat, and learn how to fish. I had dreamed about it for 25 years. But I was simply overwhelmed by the odds that I was facing. First of all, I've been broke (or almost broke) most of my life. Second, I lived 1,000 miles away from an ocean. Third, I didn't know how to operate a boat even if I could afford one. This dream of mine may seem trivial to you, but it was not trivial to me. No one's dreams are trivial! Keep in mind, I've already achieved 99% of my big dreams and goals. Another thing to keep in mind is that most of my dreams don't revolve around being rich, though yours might. I've been rich and successful all my life—in more ways than one. Anyway, in early 1998 I made that dream, as I have many others, come true. It would never have happened if I had stopped dreaming about it and not planned out its successful completion.

Think of your plan as a map that will help take you anywhere that you want to go.

What would your life be like and how would you feel every day if you could say that you've achieved 99% of your big dreams and goals?

My friend—author of *What Are Your Goals?*— Gary Ryan Blair, sent me some literature in which these powerful statements were printed: "Values lay the groundwork for your goals; Goals lead to the fulfillment of your mission; Your mission leads to the realization of your life's work—your legacy."

Pretty powerful, huh?

DREAM AND GOAL PLANNING EXERCISE

WHO, WHAT, WHERE, WHEN, and HOW

Included in the last pages of this chapter is a sample of the plan I used for my life and my career. If you are ready to begin the Dream and

Goal Planning Exercise, go ahead and begin formulating your plan on a separate sheet of paper. Remember, when completing your plan, be as specific as you can.

Here's how to do it; it's easy:

Start your plan by identifying the most important of your dreams and goals, then identify the less important ones. Next, break down each dream into smaller tasks or goals. Next, identify WHO, WHAT, WHERE, WHEN, and HOW for each particular goal. Next, ask yourself questions regarding each of these words, and write down the answers in your plan. Ask yourself questions like: WHO do I want to be? WHAT do I really want for my life and my career? WHERE will all of this take place? WHEN will each of these goals and dreams become a reality? HOW will I make this goal and dream happen?

Identifying WHEN the things that you identified will occur is the most crucial element of any plan. You must identify WHEN you will achieve each goal, and set a realistic date to complete each of them. If you do not, you will still be winging it. Attach a specific but realistic date for the completion for each goal that you have identified. If you reach the goal on time, that's great! Sooner is even better! But if you don't reach the goal by the date that you assign to a particular goal, that's OK, too. Simply keep working toward the goal and assign to it a new date for the completion. Do not quit until you have achieved your objective.

Begin with a one-month plan for achieving your dreams and goals, followed by a six-month plan, followed by a one-year plan, followed by a five-year plan. Planning your life and your career this way allows you to plan out both your short- and long-term dreams and goals, which will drastically improve your chances to succeed in living each of them out. Your plan will not be set in stone. You can change it any time you want. Think of your plan as a map that will help take you anywhere that you want to go.

Dream and Goal Planning Exercise

The following represents the contents of the written plan of action I used to begin changing my life and my career for the better. As your plans to succeed increase, so will your written plan of action. Start with a separate sheet for each of the plans below, and begin planning your life and your career today.

My Plan for Progress

Name _____

Date _____

Review Date _____

This Plan for Progress is a commitment to myself, family, and coworkers that I will follow. I believe that I can and I will make a difference in my life, in my career, and for the people who depend upon me to provide for them and their families the opportunity to live a fulfilling and productive life.

Date _____

Signature _____

Witness _____

A) Exactly what are my goals and dreams for *this month*? Who? What? Where? When? How?

Follow these simple steps to create your plan for *this month.* Use a separate piece of paper.

Assign a date to complete each goal for this day/month/year.

1. Identify both career and personal goals and dreams for this month. Start with one dream and ten goals.

Prioritize each goal from 1–10.

2. Identify the one activity that will help you achieve each goal the fastest.

3. Prioritize each dream/goal.

4. Assign a date for completion of each goal/dream.

5. Go for them!

B) Exactly what are my goals and dreams for *this year?* Who? What? Where? When? How?

Follow these simple steps to create *this year's* plan. Use a separate piece of paper.

1. Identify both career and personal goals and dreams for this year. Start with one dream and ten goals.

2. Identify the one activity that will help you achieve each goal the fastest.

3. Prioritize each dream/goal.

4. Assign a date for completion of each goal/dream.

5. Go for them!

C) Exactly what are my *five-year* goals and dreams? Who? What? Where? When? How?

Follow these simple steps to create your *five-year plan.* Use a separate piece of paper.

1. Identify both career and personal goals and dreams to be reached at the end of the five years. Start with one dream and ten goals.

2. Identify the one activity that will help you achieve each goal the fastest.

3. Prioritize each dream/goal.

4. Assign a date for completion of each goal/dream.

5. Go for them!

CHAPTER 20

QUESTIONING EVERYTHING

Review & Quotes
& for Your Notes

By using the simple
strategy of questioning
everything, you can
become a more intuitive
and conscious thinker
regarding your beliefs,
actions, and decisions.

Questioning everything
increases your ability to
reason and be rational.

Why do we spend time
doing things that do not
get us closer to our
dreams and goals?

Questioning everything,
and finding the correct
answers, is a strategy
that ultimately allows us
to check and balance
ourselves and our actions.

What do I have to believe
in order to be successful?

Questioning everything will make you a more intuitive and conscious thinker. Questioning everything increases your ability to reason and helps you make rational decisions.

Why do we spend time doing things that do not get us closer to our dreams and goals?

Questions like that facilitate more intuitive and creative thinking. If you can increase your thinking ability and find the answers to your questions, then you can increase the quality of your life and your work. The result is a decrease in the amount of time that it takes for you to live out your dreams and your goals, to become successful.

Try asking yourself these questions and finding the answers to them:

What do I have to believe in order to be successful?

Is what I am doing (my actions) working to get me closer to my dreams and goals?

Is what I believe right or wrong?

What can I do right now to get me closer to my dreams and goals and make a difference in the quality of my life?

What decisions do I have to make today regarding my pursuit of success?

When you start asking the right questions, eventually you'll get the right answers!

Is what I am doing (my actions) working to get me closer to my dreams and goals?

Is what I believe right or wrong?

What can I do right now to get me closer to my dreams and my goals and make a difference in the quality of my life?

What decisions do I have to make today regarding my pursuit of success?

CHAPTER 21

HUMBLE THINKING FOR SUCCESS

Review & Quotes
& for Your Notes

Humble thinking. I think I learned this lesson the hard way. Yeah, there are some arrogant people that are successful on this planet, but I believe that most of the people who are extremely successful are truly humble. Being truly humble is one of the many lessons that can help each and every one of us.

Most successful people
do not consider their
achievements to be
extraordinary.

I have found that successful people do not brag about their success. They do not brag about how much money that they have; it is easy for others to see that they are wealthy. Successful people do not flaunt their expensive toys; they maintain them impeccably. They do not think that they are better than anyone else. Successful people do not consider their achievements to be extraordinary. They do not think that they are the best at what they do; they believe that they simply do their job well and doing so allows them to afford a certain lifestyle.

They believe that they
simply do their job well,
and doing so allows them
to afford the lifestyle that
they have chosen.

I've also found that successful and happy people perceive their success differently than those who are not. Successful people appreciate everything that they have accomplished. They are proud of what they have and what they have accomplished. Their perceptions of their work? Simple. Their work is nothing fantastic or out of the ordinary. Rather, their work and their accomplishments are what they do to make a living. Their work is, simply, their work. Fame and fortune that accompany success? The rewards for what they do well.

Why don't they flaunt their success and brag about how much money they have? They don't have to. It is clearly evident for everyone, including themselves, to see that they are successful. They do not have to brag.

They think of their work and their accomplishments as they they do to make a living and nothing more.

They are comfortable with the humble fact that for all their hard work and sacrifices, they can look themselves in the face and say, "I made it."

Here's a short story about a gentleman that I have known for many years, and who is a long-time friend of mine. His name is Bill. He's another Bill that I know; there are two Bills in this book. Anyway, he has been very successful in his career and his life, and he has been a great role model for me over the years. He began as a salesperson some years ago and currently is the chairperson for one of the most successful companies on the planet.

When I was a kid, I worked for Bill during the summer, doing all sorts of odd jobs, like starting his motorcycle every Spring or planting apple trees in the orchard that he, my father, and their friends built. I always enjoyed working for him. He had a way of being very strong, yet fair; fun, yet highly focused on the task at hand. I did not understand how a successful man like Bill could act like just an ordinary man, when actually he was anything but ordinary. I thought that it was OK to flaunt expensive toys and brag about the wealth that usually accompanies success. I was wrong again. Not once did he ever seem to brag about his accomplishments or flaunt his expensive toys. Consequently, I never

I owe very much to a more simple and humble way of thinking.

felt threatened by him in any way, as I have from other successful people. I am proud to call him my friend. After some careful and calculated thinking on my part, I understand today that it is his humble approach to his life and his career that I now identify with and admire.

My greatest mentor regarding humble thinking is undoubtedly my father. He's not perfect, but he cares about other people and loves his family and friends. My father was, and still is, one of the best salespeople I have ever had the pleasure to know and work with. He is the kind of guy that seems to know everybody no matter where he goes, and everybody seems to fall in love with him.

My father tried to guide me to a more humble way of thinking and living. He would often tell me: "I was successful, son, because I cared for other people, and I helped other people." I did not take the time to understand what he was trying to tell me. For that, I feel like a fool. It was obvious to him that I bragged and lied about my trivial successes more in a single minute than any one person should in a lifetime. It is also evident to me, now. I guess as I write this page I am beginning to fully understand exactly why my father was so successful. Like our mutual friend Bill, it was obviously his humble thinking and his commitment to helping others that made him successful and loved wherever he went. By the way, I now listen to humble messages from my father.

I began to understand what humble living and thinking meant after I took about a year off from everything and got to know myself a little better. Then, I made the decision to start *Top of the Hill*. One of the first accomplishments that I made was the successful production of a motivational audiotape entitled *In Pursuit of Success... Eight Strategies to the Top!* Incidentally, this book contains those eight strategies. Can you identify them?

I made an appointment to sell the tape to a local bookstore. But I was sort of nervous because I did not even have the finished product with me. They were shipped a week too late, but I had already made the appointment to make the sales call, so I decided to go through with it anyway.

A day later, I found myself walking into the store with nothing but a color proof of what the tape looked like and a prerecorded copy on a cassette from the studio where I had recorded it. This was my first chance at selling a Joe Hill, *Top of the Hill* product, and it was a big step toward my future success. I almost passed out when the buyer asked me, "How do I get them, and how many do I have to buy?"

The buyer then smiled at me and said, "Ten copies will be great to start with." I closed the call with an order for ten tapes and headed back out to the car. I will never forget the excitement that I felt as I walked out of that store with an order. I was so excited that I could hardly refrain from screaming *yah-hoo!*

I had only sold ten tapes (hardly enough revenue to retire on), but it was my first sale and, man, was I pumped up.

Later that day, I remember calling my dad to share the good news about the sale of my tape and to say hello. I guess I really called him to brag, again. I remember my father saying to me, "Good job, son. Don't stop now; you are on your way. So, what else is happening?" This was pretty startling to me. I thought that selling those tapes was a big deal. Obviously, he did not think so. He knew that selling tapes to bookstores was going to be a part of my training career and nothing more. No big deal.

Later that evening, I was basking in the glory of the events surrounding the sale of the tapes, and I gradually began to realize what my dad meant. The biggest dream in my life had come true. I had become a successful author, motivational speaker, and sales trainer. Although I had not broken any sales records or made any money to speak of, for the first time in a long, long, long time, I actually felt successful. It was incredibly humbling just to know that someone valued what I had to say regarding success and motivation enough to put my tape up for sale in their bookstore. This event may seem insignificant to you. However, at the single moment that I made my first sale, for the first time I truly and honestly felt humble and successful at the same time. I have dedicated my life to seeking more of these feelings.

The experience was humbling for me because I finally did realize that, in fact, the sale of the audiotapes was no big deal. I was *supposed* to have my motivational tape for sale in bookstores. Not for bragging rights, but because it was simply the next logical step to producing a motivational tape. Having a product available for sale in a bookstore for everyone to see was simply an avenue to generate revenue and to help other people, nothing more.

Today, I got a copy of *The Employment News*, a local magazine aimed at anyone seeking employment in the Ohio/No. Kentucky area of this great country of ours. In it, there is an article I wrote regarding the presentation of can do and will do qualities in an interview. There was also a picture of me, and a little write-up about my work. I picked up a couple of extra copies for my personal scrapbook and filed them away with the others. Like most other ego-driven stuff, it has its place.

In the past, I would have made a big deal out of having my work published and my picture in a magazine. I would probably have called everyone I know just to brag about the article. Today, however, the article is nothing more than another one of the avenues that I must utilize in order to promote what I call my work and to help other people, nothing more. They are hardly worth bragging about, but they are fun for me to write.

Although it is sometimes hard to be humble, I believe that this is a success necessity.

Will you be taking a humble approach toward success tomorrow?

Although it is sometimes hard to be humble, I believe that this is a success necessity.

TAKING ACTION!

Do something! Do anything! Doing anything is better than doing nothing!

In *Success!* Michael Korda (p. 81) says: "Most of us fail because we delay tackling the jobs that would win recognition. We are held back by simple laziness, which produces a kind of permanent inertia, if it's allowed to fester."

What is it that motivates us to take action, to do something? What is it that keeps you from taking action?

What you believe directly affects your ability to take action and the action that you take is proportionate to your beliefs. For example, if you believe that you cannot do something, you probably will not even attempt to try it. However, if you do believe that you may be able to do something, you will be motivated to take the action that's necessary to become successful at it.

Success and our accomplishments, both at work and at home, can only be measured by our actions. How do you measure success?

It's what we *do* that makes us successful, not what we talk about doing. There is only one thing that I am truly afraid of. It's not living up to my true potential. There are many things that I want to do before I die and leave this planet. In order for me to do them, I have to eliminate my fear of taking action and just do them, which I have. For example, I want to try skydiving, so I bought some tickets, and I am going to do it this summer. I would like to go on a walk around the world, and I would like to have several children. These are things I identified that I want to do; I will do. I am no longer afraid.

Here's the point. Each of us only has a limited amount of time to try to enjoy life as we know it, and what we do with the time that we have left is crucial. The only things that we can take with us are our memories of the people whom we love, our accomplishments, and the fun that we had. I do not want to grow old knowing that I wasted the little time that I have being afraid of doing things. I refuse to sit around second-guessing myself and wondering "what if" for the rest of my life in some old folks home. What about you? Waiting to take action is futile.

What are you waiting for, a miracle?

Many people wait a long time for a miracle to happen. Miracles rarely ever happen. By the time we realize that a miracle is not going to happen, it is often too late. Actual miracles are made by taking action.

I've been guilty of waiting for some big deal to come along and help me get out of debt, or help me buy a Mercedes that I've dreamed of, or whatever. I've talked, wished, and hoped about getting the things that I want, rather than actually doing something in order to achieve my goals and dreams; the result is that nothing ever happens. Have you? Hope is good, and it can keep you going through tough times; but

"What the mind can believe, the mind can achieve."
—Napoleon Hill, *Success Through a Positive Mental Attitude*

The more that you believe you can do something, the more action that you will take to do it.

Success and our accomplishments, both at work and at home, can be measured only by our actions.

It's what we do that makes us successful, not what we talk about doing.

Each of us has only a limited amount of time to enjoy life as we know it; what we do with the time that we have is crucial.

Waiting to take action is futile.

By the time we realize that a miracle is not going to make us successful, it is often too late.

hope alone is not enough to make you successful. You must take action and do something.

Taking action takes courage!

Taking action takes courage!

Yes. I know that taking action takes courage. Courage is something that I lacked for many years. I was simply afraid to take action or risks in order to be successful. Do you lack the courage to take action?

We talk and wish about the things that we want, like fame, fortune, a new house or car, rather than actually doing something in order to achieve those goals and dreams.

We can increase our courage by doing the following:

- Intuitively and consciously getting to know who we really are and making a clearly defined plan for our dreams and goals.

- Improving our self-esteem. It is critically important to feel good about ourselves.

Then we continue to hope, wish, or simply talk about how we are going to have all of the things that we want in life, but nothing ever happens.

- Learning how to have fun! Life and becoming successful are supposed to be fun! We are not here to be miserable workhorses.

- Strengthening your belief in yourself, and creating a mission for your life.

- Clearing our conscience of our wrongdoings, and emptying our mental trash cans.

Taking action takes having a plan of action!

For most of us, miracles do not just happen; miracles are made by taking action.

Without a simple plan, we are winging it! If we wing it, we go into the "unknown" in lives and careers; we are unprepared to do battle with the pursuit of success, which takes more courage than most of us have. A clearly detailed plan of action, with clearly defined goals and dreams, actually propels us to take action and reduces our fear of taking action. A plan helps us stay focused on the tasks that are necessary to complete our dreams and goals on time. No one that I know has become successful by winging it.

Do you lack the courage to take action?

Taking action takes strong beliefs!

Taking action takes strong beliefs!

What do you have to believe about yourself and your career in order to be successful?

You alone must believe that you can be successful. Your belief in yourself will propel you toward success.

Taking action takes reprogramming the mind!

Taking action takes reprogramming the mind!

Take back control of your mind! To take action or do something, we must program and reprogram our minds for success. Performing self-motivators like "I can do it," or "I can do anything," are a good start. Try deterring negative influences, listening to motivational material, which I like to call vitamins for the mind. Try learning how to reassociate pain and pleasure with actions that will make you successful. These things will make a dramatic difference in your life.

Taking action takes the ability to make good decisions!

Taking action takes the ability to make good decisions!

Stop making excuses! Your decisions dictate what your actions will be. If you make excuses for not taking action, instead of making decisions to take action, you will still have made a decision to do nothing. As for excuses? Excuses do not propel us to take action; they hold us back from achieving our dreams and goals and any real success in life.

Taking action takes the ability to question everything.

Taking action takes the ability to question everything.

If we do not question everything with a simple "why," we will never know the answer to anything, much less the biggest question of all.

How can I achieve success? Why do you want what it is that you want? Why are you the way that you are? Why is what you are doing not working? Why do you believe what it is that you believe? What can you do right now that will take you closer to your dreams and your goals?

Until you begin questioning everything and making rational and intuitive decisions, your decisions will not be based upon reason and fact. They will be based upon a guess. Guess what? Guessing is really another way of just winging it, which does not work.

I am now a person of action who is no longer afraid, but who is now safely cautious. I realize that doing nothing is worse than doing something and making a mistake, no matter what the consequences of that mistake may be. I have learned how to take action by thinking about what will happen *if I do not* take action, rather than thinking about what might happen *if I do*. I have become an action-oriented man of my word and my emotions, and it feels good.

Every time that you feel afraid to take action, ask yourself the following question, and answer it honestly. Then make the decision to take action and do something.

"What will happen if I do not take action; is this something that I would like to do?"

Stop waiting to do something, and just do something! Do not "what if" yourself to death. You'll talk yourself into not taking action and achieving everything that you want out of your life and your career. If all you do is try, at least you will know that you tried, and you have defeated the fear of trying. When you eliminate that fear, your possibilities are endless.

CHAPTER 23

THE RIPPLE EFFECT

Everything is going somewhere; where are you going?

Just as the ripples of water continue to flow after a stone is cast into a pond, our actions continue to flow through the days and nights of our existence. "There are no coincidences. Everything has a reason" (*The Celestine Prophecy*).

Imagine, if you will, that everything that you do or do not do causes an effect. Everything we do or do not do perpetuates a cause and an effect. Each cause and effect is directly related to the positive things that we can make happen for our lives and our careers. In other words, for every action that you do or do not do, there is another action that you do or do not do and yet another action that you do or do not do, and so on. This effect is never-ending, much like the ripples of water after a stone is cast into it.

Essentially, the more positive actions that we perform, and the more positive energy that we cast out for our lives and careers to those around us, the more positive effects we reel in. I have a little rule of thumb that I now live by. Adopt it if you like. I believe that it has made an immeasurable difference in my life and my

Everything is going somewhere; where are you going?

Our actions continue to flow through the days and nights of our existence.

"There are no coincidences. Everything has a reason."
—*The Celestine Prophecy*

Every action I perform, whether positive or negative, I expect to get back three-fold.

All you have to remember is that everything that we achieve is directly related to either something that we did, will do, or will not do.

Don't dish out junk unless you want to get three times the junk back!

career. Here it is: For every action that I perform, whether it be positive or negative, I expect to get it back three-fold.

So, if I were to help one person to become more successful, that person will help me become successful by three-fold. Consequently, if I do something negative, I expect to get three times the negative effect that I dished out in return.

Lying is a good example of the three-fold or "ripple effect." One lie told requires another lie to cover the first lie, and at least one more lie to cover the second lie, which makes three lies told. Three times the effect for one negative action done.

The point of the story?

Remember...everything that you achieve is directly related to either something that you did, will do, or will not do. In other words, don't dish out junk unless you want to get three times the junk back!

CHAPTER 24

STOP WASTING YOUR TIME ON THE BIG FOUR!

So many of us wonder why we're not as successful as we'd like. Then we moan and complain about it. Yet we spend our time on things that do not take us closer to our dreams and our goals of being successful and wealthy. Why do we do that?

There are four things that waste and dominate our time. These four things are:

1. **Television**

2. **The Internet**

3. **Smoking**

4. **Computers and Computer/Video Games**

There are several problems with all of these. None of these activities increases or promotes the development of relationships, nor do they increase our communication ability—two of the most basic of all strategies for becoming successful. They do not allow us to interact with other people. They actually take us out of the sight of other people and into our living rooms. If you think that you are relating and communicating with someone in a chat-room on the

Review & Quotes & for Your Notes

So many of us wonder and complain about the fact that we are not as successful or wealthy as we want to be. Yet we spend our time on things that do not take us closer to our dreams and our goals of being successful and wealthy.

The four things that waste the most of our time are: Television, the Internet, Smoking, and Computers and Computer/Video Games.

They do not increase or promote building relationships, and they do not increase our communication ability.

Net, or watching TV, or smoking, or playing video games, you are wrong.

Entertainment or Addiction?

If you think that you are relating and communicating with someone in a chat-room on the Net, or watching TV, or smoking, or playing video games, you are wrong.

Psychologically speaking, we perform these activities because we perceive them to be a form of entertainment. In moderation, any of these can be entertaining and a form relaxation. The problem is, each of these is difficult to moderate, and they lead to obsessive and compulsive behavior. I know of no healthy form of entertainment or good tool for relaxation that leads to obsessive or compulsive behavior. The fact is, they simply monopolize your time. Once you sit down to watch television or get on the Net, it's easy to spend three, four, even five hours sitting there, doing nothing.

All of them lead to obsessive, compulsive behavior.

What's worse is that they simply monopolize our time.

Let's look at how much time you could be wasting on the "Big Four."

Television: If you watch two to three hours of television per day, it means you watch 14–21 hours per week, 14–21 hours that you could have been doing other things, things that either take you closer to your dreams and your goals, or that allow for real entertainment, relaxation, and recreation. I believe in selective television watching. Rather than just sitting down and turning it on, I schedule in only the programs that I want to watch. When I finish watching them, I turn it off.

If you watch two to three hours of television per day like many people, it adds up to 14–21 hours per week.

Probably more of a negative influence on you than television is the Net.

The Internet: You can find many things that are a far worse influence upon you on the Net than you can on TV. The fact that it's interactive makes it even harder to stop, once you start. As with TV, two to three hours per day on the Net adds up to 14–21 hours per week that you could be doing things that do take you closer to your dreams and your goals of becoming more successful.

Smoking: The most dangerous of all of the Big Four time-wasters for several reasons. Not only does smoking waste your time, it can kill you. Another reason that smoking is becoming less and less acceptable both in the workplace and our social structure. Fewer people are smoking, and fewer places actually allow smoking. As a result of smoking, you are alienating yourself from everyone, except the small group of smokers standing at the ashtray outside, waiting to finish their smoke. Why do you think that most workplaces today have banned smoking?

Assume you smoke one pack of cigarettes per day. You figure that it takes about ten minutes per cigarette to smoke and get back to doing something worthy of your time. I'd say that ten minutes is pretty close; it might even be low. I used to smoke myself. Ten minutes, times twenty smokes, equals a total of two hundred minutes that you spent smoking. That's three hours and twenty minutes per day that you spend smoking! No wonder employers are banning smoking in the workplace. What other things could you be doing with all of that time?

Computers and Computer/Video Games: Computers are such a part of our daily lives today that it does not even phase us to know that we spend up to twelve hours with our computers. What about the time that we're supposed to spend with other people while conducting our lives and pursuing success? Business today is still a people business; don't let anyone fool you. I don't necessarily have a problem with computers; I think that we need them for some things. However, overlooked is the fact that we spend too much time in front

Smoking. The most dangerous of all of the Big Four time-wasters.

Ten minutes, times twenty smokes, equals a total of 200 minutes spent smoking. That's three hours and twenty minutes per day that you spend smoking!

Computers and Computer/Video Games may be even more dangerous than the Net.

It's been overlooked that we spend too much time in front of computers and not enough time in front of people.

I believe that we have to find a way to utilize computers less in areas that really need old-fashioned, face-to-face communication.

of computers, and not enough time in front of people. Computers have become so widely used as an everyday tool that many of us would rather work through a computer screen and a telephone than deal with a real person. We've got to get back to old-fashioned face-to-face communication!

Many of the games are more violent and explicit than movies broadcast on national television. That alone should clue you in, if you or your kids play computer/video games.

As for computer/video games, if you have kids, or if you yourself play computer/video games, you know that I am right when I say that it is hard to stop playing an interactive computer/video game. I cannot lie; I love video arcade games. Once I start playing, it's hard to stop, so I just don't play them often. Do you want to see obsessive and compulsive behavior? Watch virtually anyone playing computer/video games.

Computer/video games take kids out of the backyard, playing with other kids, and into the house. Many of the games are more violent and explicit than the movies that are broadcast on national television. Is that stupid, or what? Here's another thing that's stupid: parents buy video games for their kids. The kids hide in front of the TV for hours. What happens to the time that the kids need to spend with their parents? It's gone! The parents love these games because they can park their kids in front of the TV for hours and not have to spend any time with them.

I am not saying to throw all of the video games away, or that all of them are bad news. I am, however, suggesting that we take a closer look at the games that we and our kids are playing, and a real close look at the length of time for which we play them.

Now, let's think about what we could be doing with our wasted time.

Like you, I have friends that do all sorts of things for a living and for enjoyment. Several friends of mine are involved in the Amway Corp. business and make over $100,000 per year working part time. They spend less than twenty hours per week doing it, and they love it. Not every opportunity is like this one, and it's not for everybody. But this is one of the many examples of what other people do with less of their time than you may be wasting on the Big Four. Interesting, huh? What are you going to do with your time? Use it, or waste it?

Substitutes for the Big Four

There are thousands of entertaining and relaxing activities to do, and not all of them have to be work or success related; most things are just plain fun. If you don't do any of these already, try one in place of one of the Big Four. You may find one of these substitutes even more enjoyable than you thought: any sport, spending time with loved ones, hiking, camping, fishing, exercise, bike riding, beach walking, stamp collecting, antiques collecting, writing music, writing poetry, writing in general, construction, model building, movies, boating, traveling. This list could be almost endless. The secret is to find something that you enjoy and do it.

CHAPTER 25

NEVER QUIT!

Review & Quotes
& for Your Notes

What is it that makes us want to quit before we ever reach our dreams and our goals?

Do you lack the internal courage and the will to succeed?

I know what it's like to try as hard as you can to be successful at something and then have it all turn to mush in your lap. But, in the end, the one that tries longer at anything always wins. No matter how hard things may seem, don't quit. There's always a way to get on top, because there's room for you at the top!

More important than using any of the strategies that you can use to become successful, you must never quit. Too often, many of us quit before we have the chance to achieve success. I have found that, due to the laws of chance and human nature, we can be successful at virtually anything within reason, if we just keep trying, work smart, and hang in there for the long run.

The author of *The Luckiest, Unlucky Man Alive*, Bill Goss, wrote this for me to share with you:

> I believe it was my mother who first programmed my mind for success. She did so early on by teaching me never to quit. I call it perseverance.

Never quit? If anyone should have quit, it should have been me! Now, I've been through some thirty near-death experiences in my life and somehow lived through all of them. I've been a garbage man, cleaned out dog pens, been in cave-ins in underground mines, been a Navy explosives expert and a Navy pilot. I've also managed to get my MBA, break the sound barrier, and survive a plane crash. I've been hit by a speeding car, and miraculously beaten and survived cancer. None of which I could have done if I had quit.

I received my first lesson regarding perseverance when I was nine. I decided to impress my family by doing an impersonation of Elvis. So I filled up a small sink with water and stuck my head in. I was attempting to wet my hair and slick it back to make the impersonation look better. When I tried to remove my head from the sink, I realized that the faucets had locked onto the back of my head like a vice. I could not get free—I was trapped. After seeing my life pass before my eyes, I made one final attempt to break free and nearly tore my head off. Like many times in my life, I almost died, and would have if I had quit trying to free myself.

Today I focus on what I call the 'Five F's of Fulfillment': Family, Friends, Faith, Focus and Fun. These things have helped me persevere through disaster and times when I felt like quitting. I've learned that you can do more than survive disasters. If you don't quit, you can actually thrive, even when faced with a challenge as great as cancer.

We all need someone or something to teach us about success and perseverance, someone to help us learn that we must get up one more time, dust ourselves off and get on to the next thing in life. This book will help you do just that.

Many of the things that I have achieved, both in my career and in my life, have been difficult, even overwhelming at times. God knows that I have thought of quitting, daily. Mostly, I have achieved things simply because I would not quit, not because I was better at doing things than anyone else was. No matter how bad things looked, I would not give in. I would not go down without a fight, and if I was going down, I was going to go down in style. I would not let things stop me or stand in my way and keep me from getting what I wanted. Although I have failed miserably at some things, I have become wildly successful at some, because I did not quit pursuing them.

When you feel like quitting, read this!

If you think that you have lost the will to continue, you are not the first person to think so and go on to become successful!

When you feel like there's no way out, there is a way out. Find it!

If you feel like you can't go on, you are wrong. You can go on!

If you feel like there's nothing more that you can do, you're wrong! There's more; do it!

If you can't find the answers to your questions, keep looking. You'll find them!

If you feel like there's no hope, there is hope. Find it within your own beliefs!

If you can't see the light at the end of the tunnel, remember...the light is still burning; it never really goes out. It only flickers and dims once in a while waiting for you to fire it up again!

Remember, in order to quit something, you have to believe that you can't be successful at doing it.

Never quit! Never quit! Never quit!

CHAPTER 26

WORK FROM A GOAL OF HAPPINESS TOWARD A GOAL OF SUCCESS AND WEALTH

"Happiness is cheap enough, yet how dearly we pay for its counterfeit."

—Hosea Ballou

Happiness, not success or even wealth, is the most valuable of all things that we can possess, yet it is the most elusive of all possessions.

"Success is a worthwhile goal but it is no guarantor of happiness, peace or inner balance."

—Tim Connor, *The Road to Happiness Is Full of Potholes*

Happiness, not success or even wealth, is the most valuable of all things that we can possess, yet it is the most elusive of all possessions.

What would your life and career be like if you could honestly say that you are happy? Not necessarily successful or wealthy, but simply happy? Awesome may be a word that comes to mind, right?

"There is a wonderful, mystical law of nature that the three things we crave most in life—happiness, freedom, and peace of mind—are always attained by giving them to someone else."

—Anonymous

As important as the relationship between success and happiness is, I have saved this particular strategy for nearly the last because all of the other strategies contained herein have an impact on how you will achieve your happiness, as well as your success. I have used all of the previous strategies to find not only my success, but my happiness as well. Please use them to find yours.

I find it sad and unfortunate that so many of us are seemingly unhappy. I say seemingly because many of us only think we're not happy because we're not as successful as we'd like to be. Too few know what true happiness really is or means. We've become conditioned to believe that happiness is related to being successful. It's not. When you find happiness, it will be the most rewarding gift of your life. I hope that this chapter of the book helps you to find your happiness—then your success. The next chapter will help you find your wealth.

We've become conditioned to believe that happiness is related to being successful. It's not.

Personally, I can vividly remember many years of my life as being "unhappy." I know what it feels like to suffer from dissatisfaction with life. It hurts. It does not have to be that way.

As you read the following pages, I want you to know that you can be happy. I am living proof that happiness can be found—sometimes easily, sometimes not so easily. Your life can be exactly the way that you want it to be. It can be and is supposed to be filled with happiness, satisfaction, pleasure, and fulfillment. No one or thing can stop you from achieving true happiness but you.

Your life can be exactly the way that you want it to be.

> "I may not be able to accomplish as much as some others, but I can be just as happy as the next man can be."
>
> —Charles Allen

You may already be happy—
you just don't know it!

Let's find out. Are you happy? Why or why not?

Are you happy?
Why or why not?

Why are we only happy when things are going our way?

In my search for success and happiness, I've found that we place more importance upon and spend more of our time seeking wealth and success than we do on being happy. When you rationalize this, it's really ignorant of us to do that since we all know that it's ultimately happiness itself that leads us to success and wealth. Wealthy people are not happy because they are wealthy—they're wealthy because they are happy.

Hey! Why aren't you happy?

> "I asked God for all things so I could enjoy life. He gave me life so I could enjoy all things."
> —Anonymous

Here are four of the most common reasons for being unhappy. See if you can relate to any of these.

1. A belief that wealth, success, and/or expensive toys will make you happy. They won't! Of those of us who have tried to find happiness in anything other than happiness, few have found it.

Of those of us who have tried to find happiness in anything other than happiness, few have found it.

2. We confuse happiness with feelings of pleasure while we are doing "what we want to do." Yes, doing what you want to do will provide you with momentary pleasure and feelings of happiness *while* you're doing whatever it is that you like to do. *The <u>trick is to</u> experience happiness while you're not doing what you want to do.*

The *trick is to* experience happiness while you're not doing what you want to do.

3. We search for something that we already have! You were born with a sense of happiness that cannot be taken away from you. You have not lost your happiness; you may have simply misplaced it. You are already happy, you just don't know it—yet!

You are already happy, you just don't know it—yet!

4. We think we'll be happy "when" or "if" we get something that we want.

We think we'll be happy "when" or "if" we get something that we want.

- "I'll be happy *when* I'm rich."

- "I'd be happy *if* I had a new car."

- "I'm only happy *when*..."

- "I would be happy *if* I could just do what I want to do."

- "I'll be happy *when* all of my problems are solved."

- "I'd be happy *if* I had..."

Guess what? You will not be happier "when" or "if." You must be happy NOW. If you can't be happy where you are in your life right now, how can you be happy somewhere you're not? Your happiness must be and can be found where you are right now—spiritually, financially, emotionally, and physically.

You must be happy NOW.

Be Happy—Live Happy—Act Happy—for Life!

How do we find happiness? Where does it all begin?

Happiness begins and comes from within your beliefs at the critical time of making CHOICES and DECISIONS.

Happiness begins and comes from within your beliefs at the critical time of making CHOICES and DECISIONS. You have a choice whether to be or not be happy—to live your life exactly as you want to live it. Sometimes we do not necessarily have the choice to do what makes us happy, or have the things that we want to have.

Doing what makes you happy and having the things that you want are only a portion of overall happiness. Neither is reason enough to be either happy or unhappy. Either choice that you make, happy or unhappy, is a decision. The choice and decision happen in a split second. Make the right choice and decision. Do it now!

GAUGING YOUR HAPPINESS

Temporary feelings and thoughts of pleasure cycle in and out of our lives. It's normal. But happiness is a state of mind that becomes a way of life. Once you've found it, it never disappears. Happiness therefore is more than a feeling. It can't be gauged by how things are going or by how much cash that you have. Here's a fact. You may not experience wealth, pleasure, or success every minute of your life because each of them is somewhat temporary. But you can experience happiness all of your life. I have been guilty of gauging my own happiness by how well things were going. I was wrong again.

Happiness therefore is more than a feeling. It can't be gauged by how things are going or by how much cash that you have.

No matter what we do or how hard we try, life still throws curve balls at us that can produce things that we don't want to happen. Things just happen—from a flat tire to failures to death. That's the way it is, that's life and it can't be changed. Just because everything is not going your way does not mean that you're unhappy. Frustrated, yes. Angry, yes. Sad, yes. Unhappy, NO. Here's the secret. Don't let the events of daily life rob you of happiness and don't gauge your happiness by whether or not those daily events are going the way that you want them to go. In fact, don't even gauge your happiness at all—just be happy.

What Happiness Is

It's Free!

A state of mind that becomes a way of life.

Something that you were born with.

Enjoying life itself.

Thankfulness to be alive.

Smiling for no reason.

Pursuing your dreams.

Finding satisfaction in life.

An attitude of gratitude.

Laughing at stupid jokes.

Getting what you need, then getting what you want.

A feeling deep inside your very soul.

What Happiness Is Not

Getting everything that you want.

Having a big bankroll or checking account.

A fancy car.

Being better looking.

Fame and notoriety.

A Rolex watch.

A big house on the beach.

A career.

Happiness is not a "thing."

The examples of what happiness is not only contribute to happiness. They only bring about temporary feelings of pleasure, gratification, accomplishment, satisfaction, approval, freedom, and a sense of control. Ultimately, happiness cannot be defined by what you do or by what you have. They are insignificant in the big picture of life.

HERE'S YOUR PRESCRIPTION
FOR HAPPINESS

1. Choose Happiness First!
Then choose wealth and success.

Choose Happiness First!

2. Make the Decision to Be Happy.
Remember, you can't be happy "when" or "if." You have the choice to decide whether or not you are going to be happy, now! Make the decision to be happy NOW.

Make the Decision to Be Happy.

3. Assume the Responsibility for Your Happiness.
No one but you can make you happy. No "thing" can make you eternally happy. It's all up to you to begin the process of finding your happiness. Once you've begun the process, you will find it much easier to receive help from others if you need it.

Assume the Responsibility for Your Happiness.

4. Practice Being Happy for 24 Minutes per Day.
What have you done to ensure your happiness? Better yet, what are you doing to ensure your happiness? If you're really unhappy now, begin by spending only 24 minutes out of every day being happy. Don't let anything deter you from being happy during this special time. Think of these times as "happiness sessions." During the 24 minutes, do whatever makes you happy and think about your happiness. Relish that special time for yourself.

Practice Being Happy for 24 Minutes per Day.

At the beginning of each day, read the following. It will help put you into a happy state of mind and set the tone for each "session."

> Wow! I am so privileged to be alive! I am grateful for the opportunity to have what I have. Everything that goes well from here is an added bonus to my life and my happiness. I am going to share the next 24 minutes with happiness. It was given to me and cannot be taken away from me. I deserve happiness.

By beginning this strategy with only 24 minutes per day, you will find that the 24 minutes will quickly turn into 24 hours, then 24 days, then 24 years.

By beginning this strategy with only 24 minutes per day, you will find that the 24 minutes will quickly turn into 24 hours, then 24 days, then 24 years.

Never Ever Hate Another Day!

5. Never Ever Hate Another Day!

Have you ever said, "I hate Mondays"? Most of us have at one time or another. Think about this. By saying "I hate Mondays," you're saying that you hate one-seventh of your life. Do you really? If not, why say it?

If so, read this book again and stop thinking negative thoughts regarding your happiness.

Life has both a rude and wonderful way of showing us that we're alive. Please learn how to experience the vitality and the joy of living and being happy. You see, when you consider the alternative to living happy, living any other way is futile.

> "Tomorrow's a promissory note—yesterday is a canceled check. Try to collect again—Good Luck."
> —Tim Connor, *The Road to Happiness Is Full of Potholes*

If and when you feel like you are unhappy with your life, read and then say the following to yourself five times. It must be read five times for the full effect. Read it now! Don't wait! Finding happiness begins with a belief and a higher understanding of what true happiness really is.

I have used the following paragraph many times to keep my search for happiness in perspective and moving in a positive direction.

> No one but me can make me happy. No amount of money or expensive toys will make me happy, they only contribute to my happiness—they are my rewards for my happiness. I can and I will be happy. I will be happy not for the "things" that I have, not for what I do for a career, and not because I am successful. I will be happy because I choose to exercise my right to simply be happy and to find joy in living. Happiness was given to me at birth, and it cannot be taken away from me by anything or anyone. I am entitled to happiness above everything else.

Does reading this make you feel empowered? It should because it's true. Now, stop reading it and live it!

Life is a wonderful adventure...happiness is what makes it worth living. Success and wealth will soon follow.

Life is a wonderful adventure...happiness is what makes it worth living. Success and wealth will soon follow.

CHAPTER 27

SEEK OUT AND GET INTO A WEALTH-BUILDING OPPORTUNITY

Please keep this in mind when reading this chapter: it is not just about making you wealthy. Rather, it is about helping guide you toward a destination of true wealth. It's about finding the holistic and well-balanced wealth that so few people enjoy today. So as you read this chapter, understand that I do not define wealth just in terms of money. Money or wealth is a consequence, a result, a reward, and a by-product of performing successful habits for your life and your career. Neither success nor wealth can be defined by how much stuff you have or by how much money that you have in the bank. Both must first be defined by who you are, how you live your life, and by the *opportunities* you you build upon in life. When you achieve a higher understanding and acknowledge the true meaning of what success, happiness, and wealth really are, you will have achieved success and wealth.

So you want to be wealthy. That's a good goal. For you to be wealthy and ultimately successful, you will find it very helpful to acknowledge and understand these four aspects of building wealth.

1. Put into perspective the true meaning of what wealth and success really are.

2. Filling a "hole" in a market can lead to wealth.

3. Identify what you consider wealthy is.

4. Learn how to recognize a real wealth-building opportunity.

Let's start by debunking one of the most common misconceptions in regard to the relationship between success and wealth.

MISCONCEPTION

Wealth and success are the same thing, right? Wrong! Wealth and success are two different things. Let me explain because there is a major difference between the two. Many of us have come to associate expensive toys and luxury items with success. We see someone with an expensive house or car and automatically think: "They must be real successful, probably more successful than I am." However, just because someone has the wealth to buy an expensive car and a big house on the beach does not make them successful. It simply means that they had the money to purchase those items. Ultimately, expensive toys and big houses are simply rewards—the end result for performing successful habits and for living a balanced life coupled with the burning desire to be wealthy and successful.

Wealth and success are two different things.

Only a Real Wealth-Building Opportunity = Real Wealth

There are always tremendous opportunities or "holes" in any number of different markets. Holes might need to be filled with a new idea, a new product, a new way to build something, or

There are always tremendous opportunities or "holes" in any number of different markets.

a better and more creative way to do something that's already being done. What you can do to fill the holes is limitless—if you look.

Currently, swings in the stock market, financial disruption in foreign countries, and low interest rates of late all create opportunities. Your task is to find the holes in a market and create something to fill the hole. What is in demand and what do people want or need? All big wealth is built upon this basic principle. Wealth is simply built upon recognizing and finding an opportunity that has the true potential to make you rich, wealthy, and successful and then jumping on it while it's hot. Is there a market with a hole in it that you think you can fill?

First, how much money should you have to consider yourself *wealthy*?
By most people's standards today, from $100,000 per year to $3 million per year as an income would be considered wealthy. After $3 million, you move into another bracket called the mega-wealthy. After that, you move up to the filthy rich and live the lifestyle of the rich and famous. Unfortunately, there are few of us in any of these three categories. Most of us are in the below $100,000 per year category. Here's my point. If you are making $20,000–$70,000 a year, you may find it very difficult to accrue any real wealth other than enough for a good living. However, it is quite possible that making less than $100,000 per year can lead to success if that income level is a part of how you define your own success.

For many of us, $100,000 is not enough to satisfy our insatiable need for more of everything and for the best of everything. The money that you earn making under $100,000 per year just does not add up fast enough after paying your living expenses, etc., to accrue any real wealth. I know many, many people who are satisfied with their jobs and who are extremely successful on lesser incomes. However, for most of us, the problem with a typical job is that there is a salary or a realistic earnings cap involved with the opportunity, which does not provide us with a large enough income to satisfy our needs and wants. Even the best opportunities at the best companies have their inherent limits, caps, and contingency rules.

Stop wishing for wealth that you cannot have working in a low-income opportunity. If you want to make a lot of money, stop working for peanuts and get into an opportunity that has the *potential* to make you a lot of money. There is little or no potential for wealth flipping burgers. I'm not saying quit your job tomorrow; I'm saying be on the lookout for a great opportunity and jump on it when you find one.

If you want to make a lot of money, stop working for peanuts and get into an opportunity that has the *potential* to make you a lot of money.

So what's the right wealth-building opportunity for you?

Simple. It's the one that you think you can do well and tolerate for an extended period of time, and it's the one that has the *potential* for you to make big, big money, thus building real wealth.

Would you recognize a real wealth-building opportunity if you saw one?

I hope so! What I find interesting is that most great wealth-building opportunities are always right under our noses, but we somehow miss them in the confusion of everyday life. Here are some things to look for when trying to find a real wealth-building opportunity.

Most great wealth-building opportunities are always right under our noses.

- The opportunity has a great pay plan.

- It provides excellent support from management.

- It has experienced mentors available for your education.

- Whatever is being sold is in wide demand—people want in on it.

- The product or service has room to grow. (In other words, it's not being done by everybody yet.)

- It has no inherent limiting factors like a cap on earnings or a salary.

- It does not cost a fortune to get in on it—or a small one.

- It allows you to capitalize on your unique gifts and natural talents.

- It's something that you will enjoy doing.

- It has a future that is more than promising.

What would you do for a chance to be really wealthy?

Rationally speaking, you must decide that, given the opportunity to build real wealth, you'll do almost whatever it takes to get it. If you are willing to work 8–10 hours a day for your current paycheck that probably has a maximum earnings limit, would you work harder or at least work the same amount of time on a real wealth-building opportunity? I hope that you would. The result? Wealth.

Do you want to build wealth really fast? Here's how to do it.

All of us are blessed with unique skills and talents—things that we do well and that we like to do. To begin a journey of real wealth-building fast, assess your natural talents and potential and do something where you can use your natural potential to succeed, thus attracting success rather than you pursuing it. Put your natural talents to work now, today. What can you do or sell or build or manufacture or develop to invent that will be a wealth-building opportunity? I know you've had an idea in mind. Try it if you think it will work!

Here are several wealth-building opportunities that I found to be worthy of a second look.

Multilevel Marketing Opportunities

I believe that both now and in the future, multi-level-marketing opportunities represent some of the finest wealth-building opportunities available. Yeah, I was skeptical too! But, I have friends that make from $24,000 to $8 million per year in multilevel-marketing opportunities, and they love what they're doing. Essentially, multilevel-marketing opportunities are simply opportunities for making friends. If you enjoy being with people, a multilevel-marketing opportunity may be right for you. Here are the three that I like. Call me for information on these opportunities.

1. **AMWAY.** Amway has changed. This company represents a fantastic opportunity.

2. **PREPAID LEGAL.** This company sells something that most of us really need—legal advice that's affordable.

3. **EXCEL.** Long-distance and Internet service with excellent rates.

Investigate some of the multilevel-marketing opportunities. You may find one that you like.

Owning and operating a unique business.

What kind of *unique* business can you create that has the potential for wealth?

Opportunities include real estate, investing strategies, some commission/bonus-based sales opportunities, the development and sale of a truly unique product, writing books, inventing new products, and more. These are just some ideas. Keep in mind, the opportunity that you should be looking for has the *potential* for big money to be made doing it.

What is the best wealth-building opportunity in America today? It is the one that you find and develop with your creativity.

What is the best wealth-building opportunity in America today?

It is the one that you find and develop with your creativity. It's the one that you will pursue with a burning passion to succeed. If an idea like Beanie Babies can be a success, surely you can think up an idea.

So many of us want to be wealthy, but we don't perform the most basic of all strategies to accrue wealth. Why we we spend our time in dead-end opportunities that do not satisfy our wants and needs? Rather than seeking out and recognizing wealth-building opportunities, too many of us hope, wish, think, and dream about finding or creating an opportunity that allows us to build wealth rather than actually going out and living out the dream of being wealthy. If your dream is to be wealthy, then be wealthy!

There are plenty of wealth-building opportunities out there, and there's room for you at the top!

Stop hoping, thinking, wishing, and dreaming about becoming wealthy and successful and start doing it! Find yourself a real wealth-building opportunity. Don't waste your time with little stuff unless you have to. There are plenty of wealth-building opportunities out there, and there's room for you at the top!

CONCLUSION

Being successful is a state of mind that translates into a way of life!

I have learned a great deal about myself while writing this book. I have learned that ultimately, true motivation comes from a desire to want more than I have and from finding a way to get it. I've learned that motivation is a process. It's a process of clarifying my own dreams and goals with the help of a plan of action. It's a process of strengthening the beliefs that make me take action, making a commitment to my decisions and to my beliefs. It's a commitment to a healthier lifestyle and to habits that take me closer to my dreams and my goals—intuitively and consciously.

So, what does being successful mean to me today?

Being successful means more to me today than ever. It does not mean financial wealth and expensive toys. It means living every day with a sense of fulfillment. It means showing other people com-passion and helping others better themselves. It means having healthy and strong relationships with my family. It means coping with the daily events of life without letting every little thing affect me. It means loving my family and showing them my love as often as possible. It means living each and every day as if there is no tomorrow. It means having the courage to do what I get enjoyment from. It means being honest with myself and others. It means being content and thankful for what I have accomplished while still pursuing greater accomplishments, thus living up to my true potential with the help of the things that I have learned.

Here's the really big question that I have to ask myself. Am I suc-cessful? Do I feel successful? My answer? Yes. I've gotten many of the things done that I want to do before I die, and I have plans to do the rest. I have a great family, my own company, and my dream boat. I live at the beach, writing by night and fishing by day, and I like what I do for my work. Oh yeah, I'm happy. Yeah, I'd say I'm successful.

When will our intelligence equal our ability to be successful?

Words to Think About

Faith	Initiative	Tolerance	Clarity
Vision	Focus	Discipline	Common sense
Instinct	Passion	Ambition	Hope
Honesty	Integrity	Honor	Loyalty
Character	Nobility	Courage	Persistence
Control	Morality	Compassion	Generosity
Tact	Wisdom	Prudence	Fortitude
Temperance	Frugality	Justice	Moderation
Cleanliness	Tranquillity	Chastity	Humility

Use the strategies that are contained in this book to help you improve your life and your career. You have the power inside you to achieve greatness. You didn't buy it. You didn't get the power from this book. You were born with it. SO USE IT! I do hope, however, that this book and I have been successful in helping you learn how to better utilize your true potential to succeed.

"Commit yourself to a dream... Nobody who tries to do something is a total failure. Why? Because he can rest assured that he has succeeded in life's most important battle, he defeated the fear of trying."   —Robert H. Schuller

Join me on a quest, a quest to be our personal best! Use the strategies contained in this book. Use and apply its principles and its strategies.

There's room for you at the top! See you there!

Joe B. Hill

BIBLIOGRAPHY

Ballantine Reference, *Random House Dictionary* © 1980 (New York: Random House Inc.)

Tim Connor, *The Road to Happiness Is Full of Potholes* © 1997 (Connor Resource Group)

Richard Exley, *The Rhythm of Life* © 1987 (Tulsa, OK: Honor Books).

James Redfield, *The Celestine Prophecy* © 1993 (New York: Warner Books).

Napoleon Hill and W. Clement Stone, *Success through a Positive Mental Attitude* © 1960 (New York: Prentice Hall) © 1988 (New York: Simon & Schuster).

Michael Korda, *Success* © 1977 (New York: Success Research Corp).

Mark McCormack, *What They Don't Teach You at Harvard Business School* © 1984 (New York: Bantam Books).

Michael Misita, *How to Believe in Nothing and Set Yourself Free* © 1994 (Malibu, CA: Valley of the Sun Publishing).

About the Author

Joseph Branson Hill

Joe B. Hill, Speaker, Success Consultant, radio talk show host, and author of the best-selling book, *In Pursuit of Success*, spent 12 years as a multimillion dollar professional salesman studying human nature, psychology, and personal development. His life's goal is to be the self-help expert to the world! Joe has developed 25 sales and personal development programs that help others succeed and conducts 100 seminars per year. His book, workshops, and seminars have gotten him rave reviews.

His experience ranges from being one of the nation's top sales representatives for Hill-Rom, a Fortune 500 company manufacturer of capital hospital equipment, to serving as National Sales Manager of Accu-counter, Inc., a company that produced the world's first firearm monitoring device, where Joe developed and implemented a national and international program from the ground floor in just three months.

Joe has copywritten more than 25 sales training and self-improvement programs in his career as a professional in the field of self development and is regarded as one of the world's leading authorities on personal development and selling. He has performed more than 300 seminars/workshops. He's the author of the 1997 best-selling audiotape entitled, "In Pursuit of Success... 8 Strategies To The Top! How to change your life, your habits, and achieve all your dreams and goals with long-term success!" This book, *In Pursuit of Success*, is a follow-up to the audiotape. He's the author of "Strategic Customer Focused Selling," a self-training sales training program. Both of Joe's workshops, "In Pursuit of Success" and "Strategic Customer Focused Selling," have been taught and approved by Northern Kentucky University and the University of Cincinnati for curriculum content.

He resides on beautiful Amelia Island, Florida, with his wife, Pat, and their golden retriever, Gus.